Creative Collaboration

Simple Tools for Inspired Teamwork

**Bruce Honig and
Alain Rostain**

A Fifty-Minute™ Series Book

Creative Collaboration
Simple Tools for Inspired Teamwork

**Bruce Honig and
Alain Rostain**

CREDITS:
Senior Editor: **Debbie Woodbury**
Editor: **Ann Gosch**
Assistant Editor: **Genevieve Del Rosario**
Production Manager: **Judy Petry**
Design: **Nicole Phillips**
Production Artist: **Rich Lehl**
Cartoonist: **Ralph Mapson**

© 2003 Crisp Publications, Inc.
Printed in the United States of America by Von Hoffmann Graphics, Inc.

www.crisplearning.com

03 04 05 06   10 9 8 7 6 5 4 3 2

Library of Congress Catalog Card Number 2003105054
Honig, Bruce and Alain Rostain
Creative Collaboration
ISBN 1-56052-687-4

Learning Objectives For:

CREATIVE COLLABORATION

The objectives for *Creative Collaboration* are listed below. They have been developed to guide you, the reader, to the core issues covered in this book.

THE OBJECTIVES OF THIS BOOK ARE:

❑ 1) To explain the place of idea generation in the team creative process

❑ 2) To introduce quick and easy ways to warm up a team or group before embarking on a creative activity, such as strategic planning, problem solving, visioning, or product development

❑ 3) To present structured processes for generating effective ideas for products, plans, or business needs of any kind

❑ 4) To provide tools for enhancing the creative performance of organizational groups and teams

About the Authors

Bruce Honig is principal and founder of Honig IdeaGuides, a facilitation, training, and consulting group specializing in the development of individual creativity, group collaboration, strategic innovation, and teamwork. Bruce has focused his 23 years of consulting experience on the development of organizational creativity and team collaboration.

Bruce holds a B.A. degree in educational philosophy and an M.A. in educational psychology and curriculum design. He conducted research in creative behavior and design at Farwest Laboratories for Educational Research and Development in San Francisco. Using a systems approach, he developed a theory and program for promoting creative action that later became the basis for his consulting firm.

His unique understanding of the creative process led him to invent a nationally marketed board game, *CREATE: The Game that Challenges and Expands Your Creativity,* and many other games, such as Just Imagine and Sproooing. He edited and wrote "The CreativeMind," a newsletter devoted to supporting innovation in business, and has authored numerous journal articles on the art of creativity.

Alain Rostain is the founder and principal of Creative Advantage, a strategic innovation consulting firm. His work has centered on helping clients create business value through the successful implementation of new ideas. He is an expert at creative thinking and the use of improvisational theater techniques for individual and group effectiveness.

Alain received his undergraduate and graduate degrees in Artificial Intelligence from Yale University, where he focused on using computers to model and understand creative thinking in people. After being introduced to improvisational theater in 1990, Alain saw the potential benefits of using improv techniques to develop and support creative thinking and effective performance. Based on this premise, he founded Creative Advantage in 1993. His firm has serviced dozens of Fortune 500 clients since.

Most recently, Alain founded the Association for the Advancement of Improvisation in Business, the first professional association to bring together practitioners across the globe (http://www.improvinbiz.org).

For information about facilitation, workshops, and presentations based on this book, contact:

Bruce Honig
Honig IdeaGuides
San Francisco Bay Area, Calif.
415-479-5102
www.ideaguides.com
info@ideaguides.com

or

Alain Rostain
Creative Advantage
San Francisco Bay Area, Calif.
888-467-7684
www.creativeadvantage.com
alain@creativeadvantage.com

How to Use This Book

This *Fifty-Minute™ Series Book* is a unique, user-friendly product. As you read through the material, you will quickly experience the interactive nature of the book. This particular book contains over sixty activities you can use in group situations to break the ice, get the team warmed up, and start the creative juices flowing.

Crisp Learning *Fifty-Minute™ Books* can be used in a variety of ways. Individual self-study is one of the most common. However, many organizations use *Fifty-Minute* books for pre-study before a classroom training session. Other organizations use the books as a part of a systemwide learning program—supported by video and other media based on the content in the books. Still others work with Crisp Learning to customize the material to meet their specific needs and reflect their culture. Regardless of how it is used, we hope you will join the more than 20 million satisfied learners worldwide who have completed a *Fifty-Minute Book*.

Preface

We have all heard the expression "two heads are better than one." The benefits of getting people to generate and share ideas together are clear:

➤ Diverse perspectives lead to better decisions

➤ More ideas increase the odds that your team will come up with better solutions

➤ When all the key players are working together there's greater buy-in and involvement

But how do you get people to share and generate ideas together—and creative ones at that? How do you maximize the value of team collaboration while minimizing the drawbacks of meetings? How do you generate ideas as a team and ensure that everyone is heard and that the team's collective wisdom is used?

This book will give you the tools to tap into your team's creativity, maximize participation, and achieve greater productivity. You can use these easy-to-follow instructions to design your team meetings involving idea generation. The result will be greater collaboration and creativity. The tools will guide you and your team in:

➤ Generating creative ideas

➤ Unleashing the team creative spirit

➤ Maximizing everyone's creative fulfillment

➤ Increasing the energy level and fun quotient at your meetings

➤ Ensuring that all team members contribute

➤ Maximizing the team performance

➤ Building the team by improving teamwork and communication skills

When do you use these tools? Whenever you have a group of people and your goal is to come up with great ideas: at executive retreats, product development sessions, training programs, and strategic planning and visioning sessions.

We wish you success in inspiring your teams toward more creative collaboration!

Bruce Honig   Alain Rostain

Acknowledgments

Some of the activities in this book have been adapted from improvisational theater games. We'd like to thank the many teachers who helped create this body of public work.

Contents

Part 2: Idea Generation Tools: Maximize Creative Output

Part 3: Energizers: Reinvigorate the Group and Increase Focus

INTRODUCTION

2

The Team Creative Process

Creative collaboration—generating ideas in teams—involves much more than just getting a group together and brainstorming. As this book's subtitle indicates, the objective is *inspired* teamwork. And that is where the *team creative process* comes into the picture. As you can see from the following diagram, this process typically involves four basic steps: Focus, Ideate, Decide, and Act. This section introduces you to each step, but the focus of the book is the ideate stage.

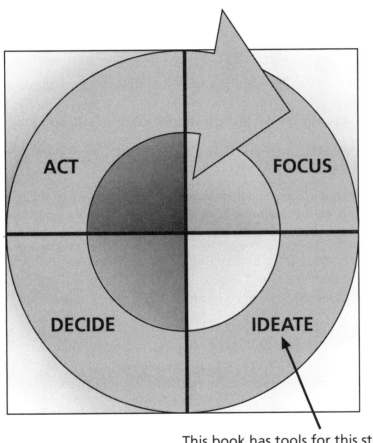

This book has tools for this step of the creative process

The Team Creative Process

Focus

Before generating ideas, it is important to determine what ideas you are looking for and create a *challenge question*. This is what happens in the focus step. A challenge question is one that defines the challenge, problem, or project in a *clear, specific,* and *accurate* way. For the sake of innovation, the challenge question should invite more than one answer. It should start with one of the following:

"How can we..."

"What are ways to..."

"How might we..."

...and end with a goal. This question will be used to *focus* the ideate step.

Teams often bypass focus, but it is the most critical step. It determines what ideas to generate.

For example, suppose a team tries to solve the following challenge:

A mother loves to celebrate the holidays in unique and memorable ways. But she is getting on in age. She is trying to get her decorations down from a high shelf in the garage, but because of her bad back, she can't reach up to lower them.

A typical first response from a team might be "use a stepladder." Although it's true that a stepladder is a possible solution to her reaching the decorations, it is important to look at this challenge in more depth to get at the "real" problem.

Ask, "What is the mother's real need?" Is it to reach the decorations? Sure. But isn't it also to celebrate the holidays in unique and memorable ways? Yes. This "higher level" need of creating a unique and memorable holiday is what is prompting the mother to decorate the house in the first place.

The team could brainstorm solutions all day to help the mother reach her ornaments. But what if the team refocused the problem to "How could the mother and her family make the holidays unique and memorable?" Then a different level of ideas and solutions could be generated. One such idea would be to go to a special Broadway show with the whole family. This new idea speaks to a higher level of need, which may be most appropriate. If you generate ideas to a challenge at a need too low, you might be missing the opportunity to generate many "great" ideas.

Conclusion: Focus is critical to generating valuable ideas that solve the right problems.

Good challenge questions	Bad challenge questions
How might we improve our customer service system?	Determine if our customer service system is adequate.
How can we make the BBQ experience easier to clean up afterward?	Develop a new BBQ product.
What are ways to increase enthusiasm among our customers?	Come up with a way to make my customers more enthusiastic.
How might we find more customers?	Let's develop a marketing plan.

Bad challenge statements lack specificity, are not open-ended, and do not ask for lots of ideas.

Ideate

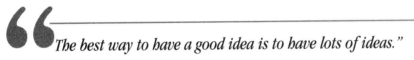

"The best way to have a good idea is to have lots of ideas."

–Linus Pauling

The ideate step–idea generation–is the focus of this book. Your team is finished with this stage when it has generated *enough ideas* from which to find a few "jewels." Unfortunately, there is no science to determining when your team has generated enough ideas. The only guide you have is to examine the ideas and ask, "Do we have enough potentially great ideas to work with?"

Note that the other steps of the team creative process also can involve idea generation. For example, one way to come up with a good focus statement is to generate lots of challenge questions, or ideas for the focus.

Decide

The purpose of this step is to organize ideas, reduce the number of ideas, and come up with the best idea. This involves taking lots of ideas and then:

➤ Discussing them   ➤ Sorting them

➤ Adding more   ➤ Merging them

➤ Refining them   ➤ Finding the best ones

Keep it simple: Whichever process you use with the group to make the decision, keep the process simple and easy to understand to avoid confusion.

Be clear on the criteria for selection: Before your group starts to "merge" and "vote" on the ideas, make sure that everyone is in agreement about the criteria for selecting the best idea. Be specific.

Equal votes: Everyone must have a "say" in the decision. This way you will achieve greater buy-in for whatever the decision is. You will also get different perspectives, which typically results in superior decision-making.

Allow for intuition: Allow people to express what their "inner voices" are saying about the ideas. Create a means to do this without judgment. Make use of all concerns. When this happens, better ideas rise to the top.

Act

Once it has been decided which idea, or ideas, will be pursued, the team must create an action plan. The plan is a map of how to implement the idea. The result of act is a clear picture of who will do what by when, the first step toward successfully implementing your idea.

Do not leave it up to chance: Do not assume that the "great" ideas your team selected will automatically be implemented. Spend time determining what tasks need to be done and who will do them.

Assign someone: You may decide some tasks need to be done by two or more people. But only one person should be made responsible for making sure the task gets done.

Determine success: As a group, decide on what would determine a successful implementation of the idea.

Idea Generation Tools

Now you understand that there is more to the team creative process than simply generating ideas. Ideation must come after the team has determined the kinds of ideas you are looking for—ideas that will solve the right problem. Once you have your challenge question in mind, however, your team is ready to start generating and innovating ideas. To assist your team in this second stage of the team creative process, this book presents three kinds of tools:

➤ Warm-ups to get the creative juices flowing

➤ Idea generation tools to maximize creative output

➤ Energizers that reinvigorate the group and increase group concentration

Let's look at these tools in more detail to understand the workings of each in the ideate stage.

Warm-ups

A warm-up is an activity that gets your group's creative juices flowing, thus helping to create the mind-set for generating ideas. Using these warm-ups will promote and support lateral, generative, and divergent thinking. In other words, they will help your group think "out of the box" and get ready to generate lots of ideas. They are also just plain fun.

Warm-ups are:

➢ **Quick to explain.** Only a few statements should be required to get a warm-up going. It is always a good idea to include an example. Warm-ups can last anywhere from two to 20 minutes.

➢ **Easy to do.** Make sure the activity is one everyone can do easily.

➢ **Winners for everyone.** No one should feel like a "losers" in a warm-up.

➢ **Involving.** Everyone should have a chance to be part of the warm-up.

➢ **Not forced.** Team members should have the option to contribute. Don't make a team member feel bad for not wanting to "play."

Idea Generation Tools

These tools are used to generate lots of ideas. Their purpose is to maximize creative output—answers to a problem or challenge. The more ideas generated, the greater the possibility of finding the "great idea." Quantity breeds quality.

There are three basic kinds of idea generation tools:

> ➤ **Collecting ideas tools:** Tools for gathering ideas generated outside the meeting time

> ➤ **"Low hanging" idea tools:** Tools for getting top-of-mind ideas

> ➤ **"Out of the box" idea tools:** Tools for getting people to think outside of their ordinary patterns to generate more creative ideas

The key guidelines typically include the following:

> ➤ No judging (of group or self)

> ➤ "Free wheeling" is encouraged

> ➤ Quantity is wanted (go for quantity, not quality)

> ➤ Combining and improving on other ideas (piggybacking) is encouraged

Hints on using tools: Allow time up front for people to generate ideas individually before embarking on group time. This is especially helpful for analytical thinkers and those who prefer some time to "process" information. It also prevents groupthink.

Energizers

An energizer is an activity that reinvigorates the group and increases focus. Use an energizer when you feel the group is less able to do the tasks because people seem to be tired or lacking enthusiasm. If energy is low, it is often best to stop a meeting to insert an energizer, to increase the group's productivity. You can also use an energizer to close a meeting on a high note.

Just like warm-ups, energizers should:

➤ Be quick to explain

➤ Be easy to do

➤ Involve everyone

➤ Be voluntary, not forced

14 Keys to Creative Collaboration

Organizations often openly promote collaboration, but teams often fall short. The intention is there, but the teams lack the skills and know-how to make successful collaboration a reality. The result is neither creative nor collaborative. So the question is: "How can we ensure that when our teams meet, we collaborate effectively and creatively?" Here are 14 key guidelines for you and your teams:

1 **Generate ideas when you generate ideas**; decide when you decide; present when you present. The three key processes that occur in a collaborative meeting are generating ideas, making decisions, and presenting information. In meetings these processes often get mixed up. One person is generating ideas, another is sharing information, and still another is making a decision. This does not work because each of these processes has its own set of rules and mental operations that work best with that process. Make it clear to the group what process you are using. This may be the most important thing you do to create a creative, collaborative team.

2 **Ensure equal contribution.** Provide an opportunity for everyone on the team to contribute to the team's discussions and problem solving. This means that when the team generates ideas, make sure everyone's ideas are heard—no idea is better than another at this stage. When you discuss an issue, everyone gets a say. This way, when you make decisions, you will tap into the best thinking of everyone in the meeting. This is not about being "fair," but rather leveraging the talents and perspectives you have brought together.

3 **Communicate all team changes to the entire team.** In a team, no one likes surprises and everyone wants to be included in communication about changes. Communicating up front lowers resistance and provides team members the option to influence the changes and decision-making.

4 **Align on purpose.** Spend time going over the mission of the team or project and the purpose of each of the group tasks. Make sure everyone agrees on the outcomes—what you want to get out of the collaboration. Your group's success requires a clear understanding of purpose. Establishing a purpose will provide the means for everyone to be at the same point at the same time, working with a shared understanding of why they are doing what they are doing.

5 **Establish a process.** Make sure your processes for generating ideas, making decisions, resolving conflicts, and solving problems—such as the team creative process described earlier—are clear to everyone on the team. With an understanding of how to solve problems and make decisions, team members can better focus on the what (the task at hand) rather than the how (the process).

6 **Record the ideas, decisions, and results.** Record the meeting results in a way that all members can literally see the work in progress. Doing this will also provide visual focus to the group. Use a flip chart and assign a recorder.

7 **Accept and value diversity in knowledge, ideas, and styles.** Find ways to get your team members not only to be open and respectful but also to actually value different points of view. Reinforce good listening. Good team listeners listen attentively to ideas and perspectives they may not like. The best ideas often come from using a diversity of ideas and perspectives.

8 **Establish team ground rules.** As a team, co-create a set of guidelines or ground rules for how team members should treat one another. These guidelines will make expectations clear. An example of a guideline might be "only one person talking at a time."

9 **Tolerate occasional group tension.** Tension and conflict often occur naturally in a team. It is also natural for a team to be in "nowhere land," in a state of ambiguity at times. Encourage members to tolerate the stress, ambiguity, and conflict. Help them realize that it is a natural part of the creative process.

10 **Celebrate.** At the end of each phase or step of a project, celebrate the successes *and* the failures. Just mentioning that you reached a milestone can be a celebration of sorts. Proverbial celebrations such as group lunches, toasting, and giving gifts should not be overlooked.

11 **Evaluate the team.** Make sure that you take time as a team to evaluate how the team is doing, how well you are meeting your goals, and how well you are using collaboration tools. Allow a few minutes at the end of every meeting for discussion, and enable your team to continuously improve its work together.

12 **Recognize introverts and extroverts.** Include processes that focus on both introverted approaches ("alone time" for generating ideas) and extroverted approaches ("group time"). Some people think more effectively by themselves with no distractions, and some like the stimulation of other people. Most need both.

13 **Pace the group.** It is important in a group to pace the work. If you move too slowly, you will bore your team members and sap their energy. If you move too quickly, you will lose most of your team members. Stay flexible and get feedback on the pace. The right pacing will differ from team to team. A good rule of thumb is to increase your pace when you generate ideas and slow down when you make decisions.

14 **Use warm-ups and energizers.** We tend to pack too much into our meetings and end up with little time to set the stage for great participation and collaboration. If you take the time to warm up and energize your group, you will get better results: more creative ideas, better participation, diverse perspectives, more energy, and better decisions.

Ready to get started? First, consider these tips for using the tools and activities in this book:

➤ Adapt the tools as needed according to your own goals and situation. They can be easily modified to fit your particular needs.

➤ Make sure that everyone has an equal chance to contribute to the activities, but also allow individuals to "pass" on a particular activity if they wish.

➤ Most of the activities require not judging the participant's answers. Make sure to tell your participants that they should avoid judging others' responses as well as their own.

➤ Throughout this book the word "problem" is used. This means any challenge or goal a group might have.

Warm-ups: Start the Creative Juices Flowing

14

Absolutely Positively............. Warm-up

Purpose:

➤ Wake up and stretch the brain

➤ Find the good in the bad

➤ See the positives in all ideas

➤ Demonstrate that ideas can come from unexpected sources

Time estimate: 3-5 minutes

Supplies needed: None

Suggested group size: 2-15 (the more people, the longer the activity)

Step #1 Choose something that is considered unpleasant, such as an accounting scandal or a reduction in workforce.

Step #2 In round-robin fashion, have each person state at least two unique things that are good about this unpleasant thing. Use this form: *"Name two good things about [the unpleasant thing]."*

Step #3 Do this as many times as you want.

Examples: Name three good things about: bringing work home, getting robbed, a project failing, business travel, a broken finger, being in the rain without an umbrella.

Hints:

➤ Use any object or subject that you believe the others would view to be negative

➤ Remember not to judge the answers

Key learning: A discussion is not needed here, but you may want to talk about how negative circumstances can create opportunities.

Any Questions?......................

Warm-up

Purpose: Create an atmosphere where any type of question is okay

Time estimate: 3-6 minutes

Supplies needed: None

Suggested group size: 2-15 (the more people, the longer the activity)

Step #1   Select someone to go first.

Step #2   The first person thinks of a dumb, unusual, or bizarre question (see below for examples).

Step #3   The other members go around and give an answer, even if it is nonsensical. Do this until everyone has a chance to answer the question. Alternatively, the question does not have to be answered at all.

Step #4   A new person is selected and repeats the above steps until everyone has had a chance to ask a dumb, unusual, or bizarre question.

Examples of dumb, bizarre, and unusual questions: Why do we breathe? Which is larger: an elephant or your smile? What is business for? How can we survive without work? What can go up and up? Do you like the bottom or the top of things more? Which is louder: a rock-and-roll band or anger? When is it best to be happy? How do you feel the way you do?

Hints:

➤ Remind everyone to ask any question that comes to mind. But also allow anyone to pass who doesn't feel "safe" asking a dumb question or can't think of one.

➤ Encourage the group not to judge the answers.

➤ If your team has not fully established a sense of trust, it would be ideal for the leader to go first and provide a model of what constitutes a dumb idea. You may first pick a general subject for the questions to be centered around. It could be related to the team's goals but not necessarily.

➤ Alternatively, you could have the group come up with logical questions related to a topic and not have the team provide any answers.

Key learning: The main lesson is that there is no such thing as a stupid question. If desired, ask the group, "How can we improve our team environment to ensure that it is okay to ask 'stupid' questions?"

Building a Better Mousetrap....... Warm-up

Purpose: Start thinking about how to improve things

Time estimate: 3-10 minutes

Supplies needed: None

Suggested group size: 2-15 (the more people, the longer the activity)

Step #1	Choose any common object or an object of significance to your group, division, or company.
Step #2	Ask the group: *"How can [the object] be improved?"*
Step #3	Each person responds with an answer in round-robin fashion. Allow any individual to "pass" if desired.
Step #4	Continue until you have exhausted the possibilities.
Step #5	Optional: If you want to continue, the next player would choose another object, and play would continue.

Examples of questions: How would you improve e-mail? How would you improve a paper clip? How would you improve a computer? How would you improve our customer service form?

Hints:

> ➤ You may want to start with everyday objects and move on to objects or processes specific to your group.

> ➤ Encourage your group to answer as freely and creatively as possible. Accept crazy ideas. Allow no judging of answers.

Key learning: Everything can be improved!

Categories..........................

Purpose as a warm-up:

➤ Start thinking in categories; good for "focus" and "decide" meeting
   tasks

➤ Warm up abilities to analyze in a fun way

Purpose as an energizer:

➤ Energize the group with something fun

➤ Get participants to learn about each other as they reveal things about
   themselves

Approximate time needed: 5-15 minutes

Supplies: None

Suggested group size: 5 or more people

There are two main variations: Chairs and Room

Using Chairs: This version is like "musical chairs" without the music.

Step #1 Get as many chairs as there are team members, minus one, and
place them in a circle facing the center (you will need open
space for this). Select one team member to stand in the center
with the rest of the team seated in the chairs provided.

Step #2 The person in the center states one thing that is true about
himself, such as "I have a cat."

Step #3 Any sitting person who fits in that category (for whom the
statement also is true) stands and takes the place of the person
in the center; others stay put. If the statement is true for more
than one person, both or all those participants, along with the
original person in the center, must scramble to sit in a different
chair. The person left standing thus takes the center and repeats
step 2. Then again, if no one stands up after the person in the
center shares his truth, the center person must start again with
another truth.

Continued...

Step #4   The process repeats with the new person in the center. This could be a very physically exciting activity. Make sure that members stay safe and don't push each other. Ask members to take care of each other and to walk, not run. Make sure chairs don't tip over. Remind participants that the statement they make in the center must be true for them; they cannot use the exercise to discover things about others they aren't willing to share about themselves.

Using the Room (without use of chairs)

Step #1   Members stand in an open space.

Step #2   Any team member states something that is true about herself and tells everyone else in that category to move to a specific location in the room. For example, a member can say, "If you have a cat, move to that side (pointing to the north) of the room." Any player can select the next category. The game continues until time is up.

Debrief discussion: What was that like? What did you learn about each other? Was anyone surprised by who fit into certain categories?

Discussions.......................... Warm-up

Purpose:

➤ Inspire creativity

➤ Share ideas and a part of each person

Time estimate: 3-6 minutes

Supplies needed: None

Suggested group size: 2 or more people

> **Step #1** Lead a round-robin discussion about some aspect of being creative, starting with an open-ended question (see suggested questions below).

Suggested questions:

➤ Describe the last time you came up with a good idea.

➤ Describe your ideal creative work environment.

➤ If you were to write a book, what would it be about?

➤ Name someone you consider to be very creative, and explain why.

➤ What are some of your blocks to creating new ideas?

➤ What steps do you take when you come across a problem?

➤ Why do assumptions get in your way?

➤ Why defer judgment while generating ideas?

Hint: Give everyone a chance to answer the questions.

Find Another Way.................... Warm-up

Purpose: Find new ways to do normal, everyday things

Time estimate: 3-6 minutes

Supplies needed: None

Suggested group size: 5-15 people

Step #1 Pick an ordinary activity (see examples below).

Step #2 In round-robin fashion, have each person state *at least one unique way to do the ordinary activity.*

Step #3 Change the ordinary activity and repeat step 2.

Examples of ordinary activities: Driving to work, telling a co-worker how much you enjoy working with him, relaying a message about a customer, greeting a customer, greeting people on the phone, sneezing, giving a presentation, eating lunch, drafting meeting notes, and so on.

Hint: Make sure the team does not judge the answers.

Key learning: There is more than one way to do things, which is required when generating ideas.

Finding the "Good" Idea............ **Warm-up**

Purpose:

➤ Practice not judging ideas

➤ See the good in bad ideas

➤ Practice converting bad ideas into good ones

Time estimate: 3-6 minutes

Supplies needed: None

Suggested group size: 2-15 people

Step #1	Someone starts by stating an extremely "bad" idea, such as "The president of the United States should spend a full day wearing a clown costume," or "let's get rid of taxes and have the government take all of our income."
Step #2	Everyone takes turns, round-robin fashion, stating one positive thing about the "bad" idea.

Hint: Allow individuals to pass if they do not have a positive thing to say about the "bad" idea.

Key learning: Ideas themselves are neither good nor bad. Their merit depends what you make of them. "Bad" ideas can be appropriate in certain circumstances. An unusual idea (which is a definition of creativity) is often is labeled a "bad" idea. A person who comes up with a new creative idea is often in the minority. Consider this quote by Henry Ford: "The Edison Company offered me the general superintendency of the company but only on the condition that I would give up my gas engine and devote myself to something really useful." Or consider this famous quote: "What use could the company make of an electrical toy?" This was said in 1878 by the president of Western Union while turning down the exclusive right to the telephone.

Firing Line.............................

Purpose:

➤ Wake up the brain

➤ Encourage spontaneous ideas to come forward

➤ Reduce mind chatter and self-censoring

Time estimate: 7-15 minutes

Supplies needed: None

Suggested group size: 3-5 people. You can have several groups if you have more people.

Step #1	Within each group of 3-5 people, team members decide who will be a receiver (2-4 senders and 1 receiver per group).
Step #2	The receiver stands across from the others.
Step #3	One at a time, going down the line, the sender fires words at the receiver, who responds with the first word that comes to mind.
Step #4	After a couple of minutes, a new receiver is selected until all players have gone.
	Senders fire their words as quickly as possible.

Examples: Sender A: Bat   Receiver: Ball
  Sender B: Wing   Receiver: Bird
  Sender C: Money   Receiver: Cash

Hints: Set up this exercise so receivers do not have time to think or censor their responses. Encourage a rapid pace by making the following statements:

➤ Don't think   ➤ Say the first thing that comes to you

➤ Go faster   ➤ Any response is correct, even repeats

Debrief discussion: What was that like? What problems came up? Did you find yourselves judging what you were saying? How were word triggers?

Greatest Dream: "No One Has..."

Warm-up

Purpose:

➤ Practice developing "out of the box" ideas

➤ Get a sense that there are new ideas and things that can be accomplished

Time estimate: 3-6 minutes

Supplies needed: None

Suggested group size: 2-15 people

> **Step #1** Group members take turns stating an idea for a potential, bizarre, and unheard-of achievement starting with, "No one has ever [achievement]." For example, "No one has ever kayaked the entire gray whale migration route from Northern Alaska to Central Baja."

Hint: Don't allow anyone to judge whether the idea is possible, strange, or has been done.

Key learning: There are a zillion things that can be done or accomplished that have not yet happened.

I Am Here.................................. Warm-up

Purpose:

➤ Ensure you have everyone's undivided attention

➤ Gain commitment to get full participation from everyone

Time estimate: 5-10 minutes, depending on the number of participants

Supplies needed: None

Suggested group size: 4 or more people

Step #1	The group stands in a circle.
Step #2	One at a time, each person takes a couple of steps toward the center of the circle and says, "My name is [first name] and I am here," then steps back into original position.

Hints:

➤ Demonstration by you, the leader, is critical to reach success.

➤ Include everyone in the room, even meeting support staff.

➤ Once the activity starts, do not coach from the sidelines. In setting this up, explain that the exercise is not about stepping in, saying your thing, and stepping out. Instead, it is about breathing and taking your time in the presence of everyone else's extreme focus on you. When participants step in, they should emotionally and mentally "center themselves" before making their statement. Once the statement is done, they should avoid pulling right out. Demonstrate how it might look for someone to "leave" before finishing the statement and how obvious this is to others. Demonstrate doing it well.

Debrief discussion: How did that feel? What happened? What was it like to be the person making the statement? What was it like to watch others? What do you notice about the group now vs. before this exercise? Was it easy to watch others? What might happen if we apply this level of presence, both in listening and in speaking, to our work today?

I Wish...•• **Warm-up**

Purpose: Prime for expressing desires, dreams, and wishes

Time estimate: 6-10 minutes

Supplies needed: None

Suggested group size: 2-15 people

Step #1	Select someone to go first.
Step #2	The first person picks a general category, such as "marketing."
Step #3	The group goes around in round-robin fashion and tells what they desire related to the category (e.g., "I wish I understood all the marketing programs").
Step #4	Optional: A new person is selected and repeats the above steps until everyone has had a chance to pick a new category, or until time runs out.

Examples of categories: Sports, training, work, speed, play, vacation, transportation, technology, entertainment, art, decoration, history, future.

Hints:

➤ Encourage your group to come up with things they really wish for, no matter how silly or "dumb" they may seem.

➤ You may want to start with a general topic, such as "vacation," and then move to a work-specific topic, like "training" or "business processes."

Key learning: Everyone typically has desires and wishes. The creative act comes from a desire, need, or wish. As the old saying goes, "Necessity is the mother of invention."

Making Connections . . . . Warp-up

Purpose:

➤ Identify how things relate to one another

➤ Flex the creative muscles

Time estimate: 3-5 minutes

Supplies needed: None

Suggested group size: 2-15 people

Step #1	The leader thinks of two everyday objects or situations.
Step #2	The leader fills in the blank using the two chosen objects or situations: *"What do [the object or situation] and [the other object or situation] have in common?"*
Step #3	In round-robin fashion, group members respond with an answer. Allow any person to "pass" if desired.
Step #4	Continue until the group has had enough.

Optional: Have the group members pick the objects or situations.

Examples of objects or situations: What do an eraser and a pillow have in common? A lightbulb and a pole? Sales and information services? A computer and a meeting room? A press release and a technological breakthrough? A rug and a dress? A hippopotamus and pants?

Hints:

➤ To make this game a little more difficult, you can use three objects. Any more than three, however, will make it extremely difficult.

➤ If you play several rounds, alternate who comes up with the object.

➤ Use everyday items or things. Stay away from comparing people and particular items (e.g., "What does Sarah's hairbrush have in common with software?").

Key learning: Things have more in common than we typically recognize. Seeing what is in common between things is an important skill for creative thinking and generating ideas.

One Voice

Purpose:

➤ Practice intense listening

➤ Let go of trying to control or lead too much

➤ Create a context of sharing control

➤ Tune in to the group

➤ Let go of ego

Time estimate: 5-10 minutes

Supplies needed: None

Suggested group size: 2 or more people

Step #1   Team members pair up and sit facing each other. They self-assign their roles as A and B.

Step #2   Team member A begins to tell a story, speaking so slowly that team member B can figure out what A is going to say before the word is completed and joins in. They continue speaking "as one voice" for a sentence or two and then switch roles, with B taking the very subtle lead and A watching and listening intently so as to speak in unison. A and B continue creating their story and telling it "in one voice," increasing the frequency of switching roles. They will get better at this as they continue, until it really does seem that neither is leading and they are speaking in unison.

Continued...

Hints:

➤ Start with something simple, such as "Once upon a time...," and go from there. The objective is to watch and listen to each other so intently that no one player takes the lead role.

➤ Let people work in pairs, then expand this to have two sets of pairs hold a conversation. Or place all the men on one side of the room as one voice and all the women on the other as another voice, and have them "meet" each other.

➤ Ask the group to "Go slowly," "See if you can together discover what word you are saying," "Give and take," "Speak clearly," "Look into each other's eyes." The intent is for the team members to completely focus on the other person and learn to anticipate what is going to be said by seeing and hearing the other person's words starting to form.

Debrief discussion:
What was that like? How did it feel?
What made that challenging? What helped?
Did it get better over time? Why?
Was it frustrating? What was it like not to be able to control it?
Were you surprised by what you said?
How does this apply to our work together?
How does it apply to our work outside of this room?

Picture This......................... Warm-up

Purpose:

➤ Exercise visual thinking as a team

➤ Create a team picture

Time estimate: 3-6 minutes

Supplies needed: 8 1/2" x 11" paper, pencil or pen (with colors, preferably)

Suggested group size: 5 or more people

Step #1 Hand out paper (8 1/2" x 11") to everyone. Have each person quickly draw any kind of line (straight, squiggly, zigzag, etc.) on a sheet of paper.

Step #2 Team members each pass their paper to the person next to them so that everyone has someone else's paper.

Step #3 Each person then adds a line to the original line to begin creating something specific, then passes it to the next person, and so on, until everyone has a chance to add to the page.

Alternatively, ask team members to make something out of the line they received in the first pass, without further passing, and then share the drawings. Repeat if desired.

Hints:

➤ Don't judge the drawings. It is okay to create an abstract drawing. Accept all responses positively.

➤ Squiggly lines, typically, will suggest more ideas to build on in step 2.

Debrief discussion: Were you surprised by some of the drawings? What do you think helped make the drawings more creative?

Quick Draw........................... Warm-up

Purpose:

➤ Warm up the creative muscles

➤ Learn or review guidelines for idea generating in a group: Build on others' ideas, defer judgment, share responsibility, say the next obvious thing, embrace failure. Don't self-censor. Let go and share control.

Time estimate: 7-15 minutes

Supplies needed: One colored pen per player, several blank sheets of paper per person

Suggested group size: 2 or more people

Step #1 Team members partner up. The goal for the pair(s) is to draw a face one line at a time.

Step #2 Each pair starts by placing two small circles on a page to represent the eyes:

Step #3 Partners then alternate, adding one line or feature at a time. Players should:

➤ Go as quickly as possible

➤ Do this entire activity without talking or giving any verbal cues of what they are trying to do

When anyone hesitates while drawing, the drawing activity is done.

Step #4 Each pair then titles its drawing by taking turns writing one letter at a time. Again, the title is completed when one player hesitates.

Step #5 Each pair creates at least two drawings, repeating steps 2-4.

Step #6 Display the artwork for all to see.

Variations:

➤ Try starting with something other than circles for the eyes or with nothing at all

➤ Quick Poem: create eight line poems in a circle, one line per person

Debrief discussion: Were you surprised by some of the drawings? What do you think helped make the drawings more creative? Did you ever find yourself trying to lead your partner? Did you feel you were following? What helped us make very creative drawings? How can we apply that to idea generation?

Reasons Why......................... Warm-up

Purpose: Practice conjecturing and developing theories

Time estimate: 3-6 minutes

Supplies needed: None

Suggested group size: 2-15 people

Step #1	Select someone to go first.
Step #2	The first person thinks of a fact, any fact, and asks why anyone supposes this is so. For example: "Video games are getting more and more popular; why do you suppose this is?"
Step #3	The other players take turns giving one new answer. Do this until everyone has a chance to answer the question.
Step #4	A new person is selected and repeats the above steps until everyone has had a chance to state a fact, or until you feel the group is getting tired of playing.

Examples of "why" questions:

➤ Most people live in a house; why do you suppose this is?

➤ Old fads and fashions seem to come back in style; why do you think this is?

➤ Why do you suppose vanilla, chocolate, and strawberry ice cream are bestsellers?

Variation: Use silly facts such as "pigs don't have wings; why do you suppose this is so?" Remember that the idea is not to find the truth of the matter, but to stimulate thinking.

Key learning: Different perspectives on why something is so provide an opportunity to practice creative thinking and to look at how things are connected. Having different people answer this question will give you a variety of perspectives on the same thing.

Sound Ball................................ Warm-up

Purpose:

➤ Focus on getting the result rather than looking good

➤ Increase spontaneity

➤ Deter people from planning ahead

➤ Keep people awake and alert, focused on listening

➤ Build teamwork

➤ Get full participation

➤ Look at the importance of building on others' ideas

Time estimate: 5-15 minutes

Supplies needed: None

Suggested group size: 5 or more people

Step #1 The group forms a circle.

Step #2 Someone starts by throwing an imaginary ball to another person while making any sound (such as "pppoooomm") as the ball is thrown.

Step #3 The receiver repeats the sound while catching the ball with his hands. He then throws the ball to another player, making a different sound of his choice (such as "wawawawawa"). That player repeats this new sound then throws the ball to another player using another sound (for example "waaaammmmp").

Step #4 Continue step 3 until everyone has had a chance to throw the sound ball several times.

Optional: Several balls can be circulating simultaneously.

Continued...

Creative Collaboration

Debrief discussion: Ask if anyone was thinking of sounds in advance to make sure his sound was "best" (stockpiling), or if people were judging sounds (their own or others). Team members should instead let the sound they receive inspire the sound they throw, or just wait until they open their mouths to speak and discover what sound comes out. Remind them there is no wrong sound. Relate this to brainstorming or idea generating.

Hold discussions between rounds. Ask what problems are being encountered. Ask what is working or what might help. If team members notice they are "stockpiling," let that be a reminder for them to listen more carefully.

Key learning: When we don't edit ourselves or judge others during idea generation, we can come up with more creative solutions.

Story Dance (Word at a Time)..... Warm-up

Purpose:

➤ Work together to create a story

➤ Note the importance of listening

Time estimate: 3-6 minutes

Supplies needed: None

Suggested group size: 5 or more people

Step #1 Start by having someone come up with a title for a story. Begin a story with only one word.

Step #2 The next person adds another single word. Continue going round-robin, with the next person adding another single word until the story comes to what seems to be a natural end or has spun out of control.

Example of a story:

"The Story of John."

John	It
Person #2	was
Person #3	a
Person #4	little
Person #5	bug
John	that
Person #2	lived
Person #3	in
Person #4	a
Person #5	big
John	hole.
Person #2	One
Person #3	day
Person #4	it
Person #5	went...
Etc.	

Continued...

Variation: You can have the team complete a poem, slogan, or advertisement one word or a sentence at a time.

Hints: The goal is to make the story seamless, with few "uhs" or empty space.

➤ Say the first thing that comes into your mind

➤ Look into each other's eyes as you pass the words around

➤ Don't judge if the story does not make sense

➤ Avoid using the word "and"

➤ Create complete grammatical sentences

Remind team members not to decide, before it is their turn, what word they will say.

Key learning: Listening when generating ideas with others will produce the most effective results.

Uses, Uses, Uses..................... Warm-up

Purpose:

➤ Practice idea generation

➤ Think "out of the box"

Time estimate: 3-6 minutes

Supplies needed: None

Suggested group size: 2-15 people

Step #1	Pick any object.
Step #2	Ask the following question, filling in the blank with your selected object: "How many ways can you use [the object]?"
Step #3	Have team members alternate answering the question in round-robin fashion, each in turn providing a different answer.
Step #4	Continue a second round of single answers if the group so desires, or start with a new object.

Examples of objects to use: Tin cans, paper clips, scrap paper, old unworkable pens, a toothpick, used tires.

Example for answering the step 2 question: Uses for an old tennis ball: Use in a carnival game, cut in half to use as a planter, cut in half for drawing circles, etc.

Hints:

➤ Allow the members to pass if they can't think of a use

➤ Remind the team not to judge any of the answers

Debrief discussion: Was it hard to think up ideas? Did anyone come up with an idea using others' ideas? Did you find any new ideas you might like to use that you hadn't thought about?

Key learning: Ideas often come from finding new uses for already existing items.

What If?.............................. Warm-up

Purpose:

➤ Explore possibilities and their consequences

➤ Visualize the future

Time estimate: 3-6 minutes

Supplies needed: None

Suggested group size: 2-15 people

Step #1	Select someone to go first.
Step #2	The first person thinks up a "what if" question starting with: "What would happen if [an unusual thing happens]?"
Step #3	The other players go around and give one answer each. Do this until everyone has a chance to answer the question.
Step #4	A new person is selected and repeats steps 2-3 until everyone has had a chance to ask a "what if" question.

Examples of "what ifs":

What if...

➤ We fulfilled all of our goals 100% of the time?

➤ We all were born with all we need to know?

➤ We all got a 50% raise?

➤ There were no more street signs?

Hints:

➤ Make sure you do not get into the "reality trap"—any "what if" is fine to use. It can be "crazy" or more "reality-based."

➤ Encourage all players to withhold judgment of others' answers or "what ifs." All answers are acceptable as long as there is a connection to the question.

Debrief discussion: How easy was it to think of answers to "what ifs"? What blocked you from thinking of ideas? How creative and thoughtful were the answers? How creative do they need to be?

Key learning: Asking "what ifs" and speculating are great tools for visioning a process. This warm-up gets people juiced to visualize a future. And practicing looking at possibilities and consequences of something hypothetical gets people ready to generate ideas.

What the Heck Is It?.................. Warm-up

Purpose:

> ➤ Look at the unusual in a usual way

> ➤ Practice generative thinking

> ➤ Introduce some levity, humor, and fun

Time estimate: 3-6 minutes

Supplies needed: None

Suggested group size: 2-15 people

Step #1 Find objects that are unusual looking (e.g., half of a tennis ball, a piece of a machine that you rarely see, an odd tool, etc.).

Step #2 Pass the objects around, one at a time, with each person saying what he thinks it is by giving it a new name and explaining what it does. The intention is for each person to give a different answer.

Example: Half of a tennis ball is passed around the group. The first person says, "It is an herb pot. It is used to hold small plants, mostly herbs." The second person says, "It is a picker-upper. It picks things up what you don't want to touch."

Hints:

> ➤ Urge the team not to be literal here. The point of the game is to develop uses that it could or might have, not to find the real use of the object.

> ➤ Do not judge the "rightness" or "wrongness" of the answers.

Key learning: Creative thinking involves looking at things from different perspectives. It is amazing how many different things an object can become. A different perspective increases the richness of everyday life. Do not limit an idea (object, process, solution, etc.) by thinking of it in only one way.

Metaphor.......................... Warm-up

Purpose:

➤ Practice idea generation

➤ Practice metaphorical thinking

➤ Make connections between attributes

Time estimate: 3-6 minutes

Supplies needed: None

Suggested group size: 2-15 people

Step #1	Think of two objects or things (see examples below).
Step #2	Ask the following question using your chosen two objects or things: "In what ways is [the object or thing] like [the other object or thing]?"
Step #3	Each person responds with an answer in round-robin fashion. Allow individuals to "pass" if they desire.
Step #4	Optional: Continue by having another person choose two objects and repeat steps 2-3.

Metaphor questions:

In what ways is a...

➤ ...team like a hair?   ➤ ...parachute like an eraser?

➤ ...president's message like glue? ➤ ...office building like a fish?

➤ ...money like the sun?   ➤ ...globe like a computer?

➤ ...cat like an ocean?   ➤ ...life like a waterfall?

Debrief discussion: How do metaphors help you generate ideas?

Yes, And/Yes, But..................... Warm-up

Purpose:

➤ Reduce judgment during idea generation or brainstorming

➤ Refocus the group when ideas are getting shot down

➤ Demonstrate the value of listening to and building on ideas without judgment

Time estimate: 7-15 minutes

Supplies needed: None

Suggested group size: 2-20 people

Step #1 Team members act as a 20-year high school reunion committee. Someone starts with a statement such as, "Let's have it in Hawaii." Subsequent players must start their sentences with "Yes, but..." Facilitator determines the length of role-play.

Step #2 Team members again act as the committee. Someone starts with a statement such as, "Let's have a band." Subsequent players start their sentences with "Yes, and..." Again, the coach determines the length of role-play.

Step #3 Discuss which of the two approaches works better for generating ideas and brainstorming.

Example: Let's have a band. Yes, but that would cost too much. Let's have a band. Yes, and we could have dancers.

Variation: Divide players into two groups. Group 1 plays "Yes, but" as Group 2 watches. Group 2 plays "Yes, and" as Group 1 watches. If desired, finish by having Group 1 play "Yes, and."

Variation: In pairs one person says idea X for the subject matter (e.g. reunion). The partner then says "What I like about that idea is X and..." and then offers a second idea to add to idea X.

Hint: Encourage the group to use statements and avoid questions.

Debrief discussion: What was it like to have your idea rejected during "Yes, but"? What was it like to have your idea accepted during "Yes, and"?

Idea Generation Tools: Maximize Creative Output

Automatic Writing........... Collecting Ideas

Purpose: Ensure all ideas are collected that might otherwise be lost

Time estimate: Depends—use in conjunction with other idea-generating tools

Supplies needed: Paper and pen for each person

Suggested group size: 2 or more people

> **Step #1** Hand out pieces of paper and a pen to each group member.
>
> **Step #2** Instruct the members to write down all the thoughts they have, without censoring them, while the group embarks on generating ideas (using other idea-generating tools). Explain that the purpose is to capture good and critical thoughts and ideas that might otherwise be lost.

Comment: This tool is effective if you have many introverts in the group.

Collective Notebook.......... Collecting Ideas

Purpose:

➤ Collect ideas outside the team meeting

➤ Apply the talents of the group without taking up meeting time

Time estimate: 1 day to 4 weeks

Supplies needed: A spiral-bound notebook or equivalent for each participant

Suggested group size: 2 or more people

Step #1 Write a challenge question on the first page of the notebook (see page 4 for how to write a challenge question). You can use the same question for every notebook or choose a different question for each one.

Step #2 Hand out the notebooks to group members and provide them with clear directions for using the technique that follows. Assign a coordinator.

Step #3 For a designated period (1 day to 4 weeks), have each member write down at least one new idea every day.

Step #4 At the end of the assigned period, have each member write a summary containing (1) his best idea, (2) ideas that may work but need further investigation, and (3) any new ideas that might be unrelated to the original problem.

Alternatively, at the end of an assigned period, you can have the coordinator rotate the books so that each person gets a different notebook for another period of time.

Step #5 The coordinator reviews the notebooks, categorizes the ideas, and prepares a detailed summary of all the ideas.

Step #6 All members receive a copy of the group summary and are given access to all the notebooks.

Step #7 Optional: The group can discuss the ideas written in the note books, develop new ideas, and decide on the best idea.

E-Mail......................... Collecting Ideas

Purpose:

➤ Collect ideas outside the team meeting

➤ Reduce the amount of time in meetings

Time estimate: Open

Supplies needed: Computers with e-mail

Suggested group size: 2 or more people

Step #1	In an e-mail, type a challenge question and ask team members to generate solutions to the given problem. Ask them to send the solutions back to you by a certain deadline.
Step #2	Send the e-mail to all appropriate members in your team.
Step #3	Optional: Compile the results of the e-mail and send the compilation back to the group members, asking them to read the ideas and add to them. This will give the members a chance to incubate the solution and to see other ideas from which to trigger new ones.

Wall Chart/Graffiti. . . . .

Purpose:

➤ Collect ideas outside of the team meeting

➤ Apply the talents of the group without taking up meeting time

Time estimate: Not applicable

Supplies needed: Flip chart paper or poster and markers

Suggested group size: 2 or more people

Step #1 At the top of a flip chart sheet or poster, write a challenge question.

Step #2 Post the sheet where all team members will have access to it.

Step #3 Instruct group members to write possible solutions or ideas on the chart, and let them know when you'll be taking down the chart.

"How can we improve customer service?"

Brainstorming—Standard..... Low Hanging

Purpose:

➤ Generate a large number of ideas quickly

➤ Intended for non-technical open-ended problems

Time estimate: 3 or more minutes

Supplies needed: Flip chart and markers

Suggested group size: 2 or more people

Step #1 Preparation: Write a challenge question on the flip chart so it is clearly visible. Select a recorder to write ideas on the flip chart and a controller who will ensure that the rules are being met. Remind the team of the four basic rules of brainstorming:

➤ Defer all judgments; no "yes, buts," only "yes, ands"

➤ Piggyback on others' ideas

➤ Accept crazy ideas

➤ Generate as many ideas as possible

Step #2 Spend no more than 45 minutes generating ideas on the challenge question. Only one idea should be suggested at a time. Should there be a violation of a rule (such as the defer judgment rule), the controller should gently point it out, then move on. The recorder writes down the ideas, making sure not to interpret or alter them.

Quota system variation: As a guide, suggest a quota for the number of ideas you want to generate. A good rule of thumb is to ask the group how many ideas they can come up with, and then add 20% more to determine a quota. The ideas should be numbered only if you use this quota technique.

Continued...

Round-robin variation: Sit in a circle (around a table or not) and ask for each person, one person at a time, to generate an idea. This way everyone has an opportunity to share an idea, although anyone has the option to pass if desired. Write the ideas on the flip chart as they are being stated. Go around until nobody has any ideas left. This approach is good to use when certain people are known to dominate the group.

Brainwriting..........................

Low Hanging

Purpose: Generate ideas independently using others' ideas as stimuli

Time estimate: 15 or more minutes

Supplies needed: 3" x 5" index cards or regular paper, writing instruments for each person

Suggested group size: 2 or more people

Step #1 The group should be seated around a table, then given a challenge question (orally or in writing).

Step #2 Members individually and silently write down on the cards or sheets of paper their ideas for the problem/focus, one idea per card or sheet. Once an idea is written, it is placed in the middle of the table within reach of everyone in the group.

Step #3 Whenever individuals run out of ideas, they draw, at random, one of the idea cards or sheets from the middle of the table. This idea might trigger a new idea. If it doesn't, then the individual should pick another card or sheet until a new idea is triggered. The new idea is written on its own card and added to the pile in the middle of the table.

Buzz Groups........................ Low Hanging

Purpose: Generate and reduce ideas

Time estimate: 5 or more minutes

Supplies needed: Flip charts and markers (one for each subgroup of 3-5 people)

Suggested group size: 6 or more people

Step #1 Provide the group with a challenge question and describe it in as much detail as necessary.

Step #2 Divide the full group into subgroups of 3-5 people.

Step #3 Each subgroup generates a list of ideas/solutions and writes them on its sheet of flip chart paper. Remind the groups not to judge any of the answers at this point.

Step #4 Each subgroup picks three to five of its favorite ideas. Encourage the groups to combine and convert "bizarre" ideas into practical ones.

Step #5 Each subgroup presents its favorite ideas to the full group. The full group is then asked to make any additions, improvements, and so on, on the chosen ideas.

Checklists.......................... Low Hanging

Purpose:

➤ Examine initial ideas or solutions to generate additional ones

➤ Generate additional solutions by asking questions or stating thought-provoking words

Time estimate: 10-50 minutes

Supplies needed: Flip chart and markers, initial list of ideas

Suggested group size: 2 or more people

Step #1 Write the challenge question on the flip chart and ask for clarifying questions. Also post the initial ideas that were generated previously.

Step #2 Ask the team thought-provoking questions or state thought-provoking words from one of the two checklists that follow. Have someone write the new ideas on the flip chart. These will stimulate new ideas. This can be repeated as often as the team chooses.

Optional: In preparation, put the questions from the checklists on 3" x 5" index cards (one per question). When it is time to use them, members can randomly choose a card, thus provoking idea generation.

Long Checklist: created by Alex Osborn, "the Father of Brainstorming"

❑ **Uses?** Put to other uses? Other uses if modified?

❑ **Adapt?** What else is like this? Does the past offer a parallel? What could I copy? Whom could I emulate?

❑ **Modify?** New twist? Change meaning, color, motion, odor, taste, form, shape? Other changes?

❑ **Magnify?** What to add? More time? Greater frequency? Stronger? Higher? Larger? Longer? Thicker? Heavier? Extra value? Plus ingredient? Duplicate? Multiply? Exaggerate?

Continued...

❑ **Minify?** What to subtract? Smaller? Condensed? Miniature? Lower? Shorter? Narrower? Lighter? Omit? Streamline? Split up? Understate? Less frequent?

❑ **Substitute?** Who else instead? What else instead? Other ingredient? Other material? Other process? Other power? Other place? Other approach? Other tone of voice? Other time?

❑ **Rearrange?** Interchange components? Other pattern? Other layout? Other sequence? Transpose cause and effect? Change place? Change schedule? Earlier? Later?

❑ **Reverse?** Transpose positive and negative? How about opposites? Turn it backward, upside down, inside out? Reverse roles? Change shoes? Turn tables? Turn other cheek?

❑ **Combine?** How about a blend, an alloy, an assortment, an ensemble? Combine units? Combine purposes? Combine appeals? Combine ideas?

Shorter Checklist: *SCAMPER,* from the book of the same title by Bob Eberle

❑ **S** ubstitute (or simplify)? components, materials, people

❑ **C** ombine? mix, combine with other assemblies or services, integrate

❑ **A** dapt? alter, change function, use part of another element

❑ **M** odify? increase or reduce in scale, change shape, modify attributes (e.g. color)

❑ **P** ut to other uses?

❑ **E** liminate? remove elements, simplify, reduce to core functionality

❑ **R** everse? turn inside out or upside down, also use of

Hint: The checklist is used to prompt or trigger ideas. The words (or statements) best used for the checklist are action words that suggest some kind of modification, such as "shorten."

Fishbowling........................ Low Hanging

Purpose: Generate ideas from a fresh point of view

Time estimate: 15 or more minutes

Supplies needed: Flip chart and markers, note paper or index cards, pen for each person

Suggested group size: 6-18 people

Step #1	Divide the team in half. Neither group should have more than nine people. Have the first group sit in a "U" shape around a flip chart. Have the second group sit behind the first group in any configuration.
Step #2	Introduce a challenge question and clarify every element by having the whole team ask questions.
Step #3	The inside group brainstorms using the traditional brainstorming approach (see page 51) for about 5-10 minutes. The second group is not permitted to talk to the first group while it brainstorms. Instead, the second group observes and writes down ideas on the note paper or index cards provided. These ideas can be silently passed to the brainstorming group.
Step #4	The groups change physical positions. The second group then brainstorms and the first group observes. Now the first group writes notes and ideas and passes them to the second group.
Step #5	Both groups discuss their observations and ideas. The new ideas that emerge should be added to the flip chart.

Hints: Why have a silent, observing group? Sometimes it is easier to generate ideas when you are not in the middle of a brainstorming session but are prompted by others who are generating ideas. This is particularly true for a more introverted group—that is, a group that finds it easier to generate ideas without the pressure of performing in a group.

Out of ideas? The first observing group may have fewer ideas when it is time for them to brainstorm. This is okay. Allow for silence, and in the silence probably will come more ideas.

Force-Field Analysis............ Low Hanging

Purpose: Generate a list of ways to help achieve a goal by focusing on the forces affecting it

Time estimate: 15 or more minutes

Supplies needed: Flip chart and markers

Suggested group size: 2 or more people

Step #1   Briefly describe a) your chosen goal, b) an ideal outcome, and c) the most catastrophic outcome.

Step #2   Ask the team to pretend it is somewhere between the two extreme outcomes in a tug of war. Some present-day forces are pulling the team toward catastrophe and others are pulling it toward the ideal. List these forces.

Step #3   Generate ideas for minimizing the opposing forces. Write them on the flip chart.

Step #4   Generate ideas for maximizing the supporting forces. Write them on the flip chart.

Hint: Make sure that the discussion revolves around the forces that exist in the present, not future forces that may or may not develop.

Example: We are launching a new product. We want it to be very lucrative. The most catastrophic outcome is that no one (or very few customers) will buy it.

Supporting forces:	Opposing forces:
➤ Broad company support	➤ A tiny advertising budget
➤ A well-designed product	➤ Extensive competition
➤ A large potential customer base	➤ Expense

Idea Gallery..................... Low Hanging

Purpose: Generate a large quantity of ideas for two or more challenge questions (problems) in a short period of time

Time estimate: 5-55 minutes, depending on the number of problems

Supplies needed: Flip charts and markers (one chart for each challenge question)

Suggested group size: 6 or more people

Step #1 At the top of each flip chart page, write one challenge question, and spread the pages around the room. (It would be even better to put them in separate rooms, if possible.)

Step #2 Divide the team into subgroups (three or more people per subgroup) and have each group go to a separate flip chart with a challenge question written on it.

Step #3 The subgroups then read what is written on the flip chart. The groups brainstorm ideas related to the problem/focus stated on their flip charts.

Step #4 Each subgroup rotates to a new flip chart or problem after two to five minutes.

Hints: Use this tool for two or more problems. It is ideal to work with fewer problems than the number of people divided by three. For example, if there are 15 people, then five or fewer flip charts or problems is ideal.

This also can be done with individuals, rather than groups, rotating and answering questions. But the group approach allows for more interaction.

KJ Method..............................

Based on a method by Kawakita Jiro

Purpose: Generate ideas from a vague challenge question

Time estimate: 45 or more minutes

Supplies needed: At least thirty 3" x 5" cards and one pen per person, butcher paper, and markers

Suggested group size: 3 or more people

Step #1 The team is given a theme or a challenge question.

Step #2 Team members individually write their ideas on cards (one idea per card, limiting the number of words per card to 25).

Step #3 The group organizes and sorts the cards into themes. Encourage a playful spirit here.

Step #4 The group further organizes and sorts the cards in each theme into more specific themes (subthemes) if they can.

Step #5 The group organizes the cards still further into sub-subthemes.

Step #6 The group relaxes and draws or writes down on one large sheet of butcher paper any additional ideas that come to mind. These ideas do not have to be related. Encourage group members to draw pictures and graffiti playfully. This step is intended to be more free-flowing than the previous steps. Using butcher paper (a different medium than the index cards) allows for a slight shift for the mind and a potential break from using words.

Step #7 Individual members read or describe what they have written or drawn on the butcher paper, while more ideas are written on additional index cards and added to the other cards.

M Brainstorming......... Low Hanging

Based on a method developed by Mitsubishi

Purpose: Generate ideas independently while making use of the team as inspiration

Time estimate: 20 or more minutes

Supplies needed: One flip chart and markers, Post-it notepads, and a pen for each person

Suggested group size: 4-15 people

Step #1 A challenge question is written on the flip chart and discussed.

Step #2 Team members are given some time (3-15 minutes) to individually write down their ideas and solutions to the given problem/focus, one idea per Post-it note.

Step #3 Ask participants each to quickly read their ideas aloud to the others. Discourage editing. While the ideas are being read, permit no one to comment on the ideas. Ask the team to write down new thoughts and ideas that are stimulated by the ideas read aloud and keep them private for now.

Step #4 Only the original ideas that are read aloud are placed on the flip chart.

Step #5 Team members individually present their new idea(s) in greater detail. These new ideas are then written on the flip chart.

Hint: The ideas created in all steps can be used as potential sources of ideas or solutions.

Matrix Analysis.................. Low Hanging

Purpose:

➤ Generate solutions using the attributes of two dimensions

➤ Develop new products or programs

Time estimate: 15-20 minutes

Supplies needed: Flip chart or notepad and markers

Suggested group size: 2 or more people

Step #1 Briefly describe a problem/focus for which you need a creative solution.

Step #2 Select the two key dimensions or attributes that affect this problem.

Step #3 On the flip chart or sheet of paper, make a two-dimensional matrix. Label one axis with the first variable and the other axis with the second variable. Along each axis, write all the possible points for each variable. Draw lines from each axis to form a table, as shown below, that represents the intersections of points from each axis.

Step #4 To spur solutions, generate ideas for each square, for those squares that seem most promising, or for random squares.

Hints: Put extra effort into determining the two dimensions and the points in each axis. This will help make this exercise most effective. To clarify the exercise, share the following example with participants.

Example: The problem is to find a new food product. Perhaps the two most important dimensions in a new food product would be kinds of food and forms of food. The possibilities for each variable are shown below. For each combination, such as "Meat/Drink" or "Grain/Topping," brainstorm specific ideas for a new product.

Forms of Food

	Drink	Concentrated	Soup	Chips	Topping
Meat					
Fruit					
Grain					
Spice					
Vegetable					

Kinds of Food

Nominal Group Technique.....

Low Hanging

Purpose: Generate ideas anonymously

Time estimate: 15 or more minutes

Supplies needed: One flip chart and markers, index cards, and writing instrument (all with same color ink)

Suggested group size: 4-15 people

Step #1 Give the group a challenge question. Ask for any clarifying questions. Designate someone to serve as the recorder.

Step #2 Hand out blank index cards to everyone in the group. Give the members 3-5 minutes to write one idea on each card. Individuals who do not have an idea can leave the card blank.

Step #3 The cards are collected and shuffled, taking care not to show the source of the ideas. The recorder transcribes the ideas on to the flip chart.

Step #4 Any member is permitted to propose rewording an item, eliminating a duplicate item, or combining similar items into one. But if anyone objects to the proposed change, the proposal process stops.

Step #5 Repeat steps 2-4 several times until an idea-generating round turns up only blank cards.

Pass It On.......................... Low Hanging

Purpose: Generate ideas individually, combining and building on others' ideas

Approximate time: 10 or more minutes

Supplies needed: 8 1/2" x 11" paper, 3" x 3" pad of Post-It notes, pens for each person (fine-point permanent marker works best)

Suggested group size: 3 or more people

Step #1 Present the focus statement to the group. Have the group sit in a circle or around a table.

Step #2 Give each team member a blank sheet of paper and a Post-It pad. Ask each person to think of three ideas and write one idea per Post-it note, then place the notes on the blank sheet.

Step #3 Team members each pass their pages to the next person (right or left). Each person then reads all the ideas on the "new" page and adds three more ideas below the ones already there. The ideas can be entirely new ideas, combinations of any two ideas, or modifications of previous ideas.

Step #4 Continue passing the sheets around until time is up or you feel you have enough ideas (you may need to have more pages in case the sheets fill up).

Step #5 Place the ideas on the flip chart or wall.

Using Goals..................... Low Hanging

Purpose: Generate ideas based on the goals of the problem

Time estimate: 10 or more minutes

Supplies needed: One flip chart and markers, notecards, and a pen

Suggested group size: 2 or more people

Step #1   Present a challenge question and have the team generate a list of goals for the solution(s).

Strive to have at least four goals; make sure they are comprehensive. The goals should be somewhat measurable and within your level of control. Make them visible to the whole group on a flip chart or equivalent.

Step #2   For each goal generated in step 1, generate a list of potential solutions (one goal at a time).

Step #3   Through discussion and brainstorming, merge and integrate the solutions generated in step 2. Find ideas that answer the challenge question and fulfill all of the goals. Write these tentative ideas on the flip chart.

Hint: When generating ideas from each goal in Step #2, remove or cover the other goals from the group's sight so the group only focuses on one goal at a time.

Arts and Crafts.................Out of the Box

Purpose: Use visual and motor abilities to create new ideas

Time estimate: 15 or more minutes

Supplies needed: Flip chart and art supplies (e.g., construction paper, tape, glue, clay, pipe cleaners, straws, scissors, markers, Popsicle sticks)

Suggested group size: 3 or more people

Step #1 Describe a challenge question and answer any clarifying questions.

Step #2 Direct each person to create, from the art materials, something that answers the problem. It does not need to be a real, workable solution. If no one can come up with a solution, have the group create something that suggests the problem itself.

Step #3 For individual art objects, ask the creators to title their own piece.

Step #4 Then have these individuals go around the room and describe their object. Write a summary of each description on the flip chart.

Step #5 Generate a new set of solutions from the art objects. Ask, "In what ways can we use the art objects to inspire solutions to our problem?"

"Bad Ideas" Technique . . . . Out of the Box

Purpose:

➤ Generate ideas based on "bad" ideas

➤ Find the good idea in the "bad" idea

Time estimate: 6 or more minutes

Supplies needed: Flip chart and markers

Suggested group size: 3 or more people

Step #1 State the challenge and ask for clarifying questions.

Step #2 The team generates, in brainstorming fashion (see page 51), unworkable and bizarre solutions for the problem, perhaps to the extent of making the challenge worse. Write these on the flip chart.

Step #3 Come to agreement about which solution is the worst. Circle the worst idea.

Step #4 As a group, generate ways to make the "bad" idea workable and write these down on a separate chart. Alternatively, you can ask the group to reverse the bad idea to generate additional ideas (e.g. The reverse of the idea of "Give everyone some money" is "Take money away from everyone.")

Step #5 Pick the next worst idea and then repeat step 4. Repeat this for as long as desired.

Hint: Mention to your group that "great" ideas can evolve from ones that are considered to be very "bad," and that "bad" ideas can stimulate "good" ones.

Example: A town had a problem with litter. The "bad" idea was to give people money for their litter. From this idea came the actual solution the town implemented—a garbage can that played musical sounds triggered by litter being thrown in the can. This solved the litter problem.

Collective Vision. . . . . .Out of the Box

Purpose:

➤ Visualize the solution as a group

➤ Create a collective vision

Time estimate: 10 or more minutes

Supplies needed: Flip chart and markers

Suggested group size: 3 or more people

Step #1 State the challenge question and ask for clarifying questions.

Step #2 Invite group members to close their eyes if they desire and visualize solutions to the challenge question.

Step #3 One at a time, and in any order, have players call out attributes or aspects of their vision to create a group vision. Instruct the group members to accept all the attributes and use them in their own vision, thus creating a collective vision. Have someone recording the attributes.

Hint: This tool is great for visioning future states.

Combining Teams.............Out of the Box

Purpose: Generate ideas from both a logical and creative viewpoint

Time estimate: 30 or more minutes

Supplies needed: 2 flip charts and markers

Suggested group size: 3 or more people divided into 3 subgroups

Step #1   Form three equal groups. One group takes the role of "logical thinkers," the second takes the role of "creative thinkers," and the third group takes the role of "synthesizers."

Step #2   Provide the "logical thinkers" and the "creative thinkers" with a challenge question. Have each group, for 5-10 minutes and in brainstorming fashion (see page 51), independently generate ideas for the solution to the problem/focus from the perspective of their specified role (logical or creative). Instruct the logical thinkers to think rationally and pragmatically and the creative thinkers to use their imagination and intuition. Each group generates a list. The third group, "the synthesizers," just listens to each group without commenting or generating any ideas.

Step #3   Give the synthesizers the two idea lists and tell them to force combinations between them. Their job is to develop new, creative, and workable solutions using the ideas of the "logical thinkers" and the "creative thinkers" combined. While this is being done, the first two groups just sit and listen to the "synthesizers" without commenting or providing ideas.

Hints:

➤   To avoid biases, it is important that the separate groups do not interfere with each other.

➤   You may want to try this with your group using e-mail. This will eliminate the downtime each group experiences.

➤   This tool is a particularly strong one for generating good ideas because it gives the group the opportunity to use the three key creative thinking approaches in a devoted way.

Crazy Idea Game.................Out of the Box

Purpose: Generate breakthrough ideas under competitive pressure while having fun

Time estimate: 35 minutes

Supplies needed: Flip chart and markers; 2-minute timer or a watch with a second hand

Suggested group size: 4 or more people

Step #1 Divide the team into two groups and select a recorder/referee who will not participate in either group.

Step #2 Describe a challenge question and answer any clarifying questions.

Step #3 Select a group to go first (group A). That group begins by suggesting an absurd or bizarre idea for the solution to the challenge. For example, if the challenge is "how to convince the CEO of the value of our $300,000 proposal," perhaps an absurd answer would be to blackmail her.

Step #4 Give the second group (group B) two minutes to develop a practical solution to the initial problem from the idea suggested by the first group.

Step #5 If group B succeeds (judged by the referee), it gets one point. The referee writes down each solution as it is proposed.

Step #6 The groups trade roles with the second group providing the remote or bizarre idea to the other group (group A) and repeating steps 3-5. Continue trading back and forth as appropriate.

Optional: At the end of a predetermined time, the group with the most points is declared the winner.

Exaggerate the Problem. . . . . . . .Out of the Box

Purpose:

➤ Generate ideas by exaggerating the problem/focus

➤ Add humor and energy to your sessions

Time estimate: 10 or more minutes

Supplies needed: Flip chart and markers

Suggested group size: 3 or more people

Step #1 Describe a challenge question and answer any clarifying questions.

Step #2 As a group, generate new challenge questions that will grossly exaggerate the original challenge question. Make the problem much bigger, harder, odder, and so on.

Step #3 Select an exaggerated challenge question. Generate a list of solutions to the new, grossly exaggerated challenge question. Use the rules of brainstorming: piggyback on others, strive for lots of ideas, allow for crazy or extreme ideas, don't judge.

Step #4 Ask, "In what ways can we use the exaggerated solutions to inspire real solutions to our problem?"

Step #5 Go back to step 3 and have the team pick another grossly exaggerated challenge question. Complete steps 3-4. Continue until time runs out.

Examples of exaggerated challenge questions: Suppose the focus statement is "How might we successfully launch a public relations campaign for a new cheese product?" Exaggerate this statement:

➤ How could we get the whole world to know about this new product in 24 hours? One hour? One minute?

➤ What would make every writer in the world want to write about this?

➤ What would get customers to tell all their friends?

Field Trip.........................Out of the Box

Purpose: Find outside stimulus for a problem/focus

Time estimate: Variable

Supplies needed: Notepads, pens, flip chart, and markers

Suggested group size: 2 or more people

Step #1 Discuss in detail the problem/focus (if you have not done so already). Then summarize the problem/focus.

Step #2 As a group, take a trip to visit a place (or places) that has some (but not complete) relevance to the problem/focus. For example, if you are working on a marketing problem for your high-tech company, visit a toy store and see how it markets its products.

Step #3 Instruct the group to carry around a pad for taking notes. After the field trip, ask the group to use (independently or together) the standard brainstorming tool (page 51) to generate additional ideas that may have surfaced during the trip. List the ideas on the flip chart.

Free Fit............................Out of the Box

Purpose: Generate breakthrough ideas through free association

Time estimate: 15 or more minutes

Supplies needed: Flip chart and markers

Suggested group size: 3 or more people

Step #1 Write a challenge question on the flip chart and answer any clarifying questions.

Step #2 Have the team select a *key word* in the challenge question.

Step #3 In round-robin fashion, have the members free-associate aloud starting from the key word only. Have someone record the associations on the flip chart. Stop after a minute or two.

Step #4 From the list of associations, have the team choose the three words that seem farthest from the problem.

Step #5 Using these three words, "force-fit" them (one or all three) into a potential solution to the problem.

Step #6 Repeat steps 2-5 as often as needed.

Guided Reflection-Vision......Out of the Box

Purpose:

➤ Use the teams' intuition to develop ideas

➤ Create a way for each person to contribute to a vision

➤ Come up with surprising ideas

➤ Use all of the senses to stimulate creativity

➤ Bring a personal focus to the group

Time estimate: 10-30 minutes

Supplies needed: Flip chart and markers

Suggested group size: 3 or more people

Step #1 Describe the problem/focus.

Step #2 Instruct the participants to sit in a relaxed position because they are about to go on a visual journey. Ask them to close their eyes if they desire.

Step #3 Speak or read a guided visualization similar to the examples below.

Step #4 Ask participants to open their eyes gently and to silently summarize what they experienced in the visualization.

Step #5 Have participants describe their experience to the group and then state the key components and ideas they came up with. Have someone write these on a flip chart.

Ask the participants to include anything that surprised them.

Hints:

➤ Make sure the environment is comfortable. Have the participants begin by focusing on their breathing.

➤ Don't force anyone to close her eyes.

Continued...

> ➤ Prepare a written visualization ahead of time.

> ➤ Ask open-ended questions that are specific enough to prompt creativity but general enough to allow for individual expression during the visualization. Find ways to access all of the senses (e.g., "How does it smell, look, feel, sound?").

> ➤ Take your time reading the visualization. Read it slowly, allowing participants time to create the scenario in their minds and to "answer" to themselves the questions you are asking.

> ➤ For best results, lead this exercise before using the Art & Crafts tool on page 67.

Example #1 Guided Imagery: At Work

Imagine it is three years from now and you have just walked into your new work area. It is everything you ever dreamed of in a workspace. Picture the area in your mind in great detail. What do you see? Who else is there? What sounds do you hear? You look over to the right and are surprised by something. What is it?

There to greet you are your two favorite "customers." They are wearing big smiles. What do they say?

Sit down. You are very comfortable. What do you feel?

Next, check your to-do list for the coming week. To your delight, the project you always wanted to do starts this week. What is that project?

Example #2 Guided Imagery: Wise Person

Imagine being in a beautiful forested area. (Allow at least 10 seconds to lapse.) Take a look around. What do you see? What colors do you see? What does it smell like? What does it feel like?

In front of you is a trail. Begin to walk slowly on the trail. Continue walking. Feel the path beneath your feet. Are you walking up the path? Are you walking down? Is the path windy? Listen to the sounds of the forest. What do you hear?

You are beginning to climb up a steep mountain path with little effort. Notice the path and how it feels. Continue to climb effortlessly. Climb higher and higher. You notice in the distance a clearing. Walk to that clearing. You are now up on top of the mountain. Look to your left and notice a short stairway leading farther up. Climb it. (Wait at least five seconds here.)

At the top of the stairway is a wise person. Look at this person carefully. Ask the person about your problem and wait for an answer. (Wait at least 30 seconds here.) The wise person smiles at you, hands you a folded piece of paper, and whispers something to you. (Wait at least 30 seconds here.) Thank the wise person and walk down the stairs to the mountaintop. Take a look around and open the paper from the wise person. What does it say?

Backtracking your way off the mountaintop, walk back slowly, thinking about the wise person and the messages. (Allow at least 10 seconds here.) In a moment you will have reached the bottom of the mountain. You have now reached the end of your journey. Leave the forest and take with you all the images and messages. Open your eyes when you are ready to come back to this room.

(You can change the scenery and any aspect of this imagery as desired. Remember to use your own creativity for this.)

Incubation......................Out of the Box

Purpose: Incubate the problem to find workable solutions

Time estimate: Variable

Supplies needed: Notepads, pens, flip chart, and markers

Suggested group size: 2 or more people

Step #1   Discuss in detail, then summarize, the problem/focus.

Step #2   Ask the group to "incubate" the problem by not consciously thinking about it. This may occur in the following ways:

➤ Take breaks from the group activity and instruct the group not to discuss the problem.

➤ Dismiss the group for the day or week and ask the members not to directly think about the problem, but to take a notepad with them wherever they go (bathroom, car, restaurants, etc.) to record any idea that may come up.

➤ Encourage the group members each to keep a "dream journal." From the dreams may come a solution.

➤ As a group, take a trip to visit an interesting place (e.g., museum, store, or amusement park). Instruct the group not to directly think about the problem, but to carry around a notepad to record any ideas that may surface.

Step #3   Immediately after the above events, ask the group to use (independently or together) the standard brainstorming tool (page 51) to generate additional ideas that may have surfaced during the formal incubation period. List the ideas on the flip chart.

Make Connections. . . . . .Out of the Box

Purpose: Generate ideas using random triggers

Time estimate: 15 or more minutes

Supplies needed: Flip chart and markers, a random stimulus of some type such as a bowl full of charms, a dictionary, or an encyclopedia

Suggested group size: 2 or more people

Step #1 Describe the challenge question, and answer any clarifying questions.

Step #2 Randomly select an object or word and tell the team what the object is (show it if you can). You can even randomly point to something.

Step #3 Review the attributes of the item or word, making sure that many attributes are considered (e.g., color, shape, function, size, symbolism).

Step #4 Have the team non-judgmentally generate ideas about how the characteristics of that object can solve the given problem.

You can phrase the question in one of three ways:

1) What does this object or word tell you about the problem or question?

2) What ideas do you get from this object or word that might help solve this problem?

3) How is this object like the problem?

Write these ideas on the flip chart.

Hint: Encourage the group to keep an open mind and look at all possible aspects of the object (symbolic, metaphoric, and literal).

Example: Suppose the problem is "improve our customer service." The random item might be "washing machine." Some attributes of a washing machine are: It cleans, agitates, goes in cycles, requires soap, is white in color. A solution might be: Create a customer service cycling process where we clean our errors.

Metaphors.........................Out of the Box

Purpose:

➤ Generate ideas using metaphor

➤ Get different points of view

➤ Capture the spirit and essence of what you are trying to solve

Time estimate: 15 or more minutes

Supplies needed: Flip chart and markers

Suggested group size: 2 or more people

Step #1 Write the challenge question or goal on the flip chart and answer any clarifying questions.

Step #2 Pick a symbol or metaphor that best captures the spirit and essence of the problem or goal (for example, if the problem is to expand market share, the symbol could be a bird expanding its wings).

Step #3 Without considering the problem, have the group list the attributes of the symbol.

Step #4 For each attribute, have the group generate ideas for bringing that attribute into a solution to the problem. Encourage bizarre solutions.

Step #5 Repeat steps 2-4 to generate more ideas and solutions.

Step #6 Examine the solutions. Improve and develop each into a more realistic, sensible, and workable solution.

Hints:

➤ You can focus the metaphor on a certain area, such as nature, architecture, physics, communications, computers, music, and so on.

➤ Your team players can choose their own symbols and generate ideas on their own.

➤ Use more than one symbol to access the imagination of all the participants.

Example: Suppose you want to improve the corporate culture for innovation, and the symbol you choose is a tree. Some attributes of a tree are: roots, seasonality, hard outer bark, unpredictable limb patterns, and leaves that breathe.

For each attribute, what ideas do you get for improving the corporate culture?

➤ What would provide more "roots" to the culture?

➤ What would give better cycles and "seasons" to it?

➤ What could protect the culture like "hard outer bark"?

➤ What unpredictability might actually stimulate the culture?

➤ What mutually profitable exchanges might occur (such as the exchange of oxygen and carbon dioxide in leaves)?

Putting It All Together..........Out of the Box

Purpose: Integrate a variety of ideas

Time estimate: 55 minutes

Supplies needed: Flip chart, markers, paper, and pens

Suggested group size: 3 or more people

Step #1 Describe the problem/focus and answer any clarifying questions.

Step #2 Team members individually generate ideas on a sheet of paper.

Step #3 Two random members each state *one* of their ideas.

Step #4 The rest of the team works to put these two ideas together to create another idea. The new, integrated ideas are written on the flip chart.

Step #5 A third person reads an idea, and the group attempts to integrate all three ideas into one solution, which also is written on the flip chart.

Step #6 This continues until *all* ideas of all members have been read and integration has been attempted and charted.

Role Perspectives...............Out of the Box

Purpose: Generate solutions from different points of view

Time estimate: 15 or more minutes

Supplies needed: Flip chart and markers

Suggested group size: 3 or more people

Step #1 Write the challenge question on the flip chart and answer any clarifying questions.

Step #2 Pick a variety of roles (as many roles as there are people in the group) and assign one role to each person. One person can assume more than one role. The roles can be realistic or bizarre. This depends on the group, its willingness to experiment, and the problem you are solving.

Examples are:

Realistic	Archetypes	Famous	Animals
supervisor	clown	daVinci	dolphin
CEO	critic	Groucho Marx	elephant
customers	wizard	Mickey Mouse	insect
accountant	explorer	Albert Einstein	dinosaur
children	artist	Helen Keller	snake

Optional: Prepare 3" x 5" cards, with a different role on each card, to hand out to team members. This makes the process more like a game.

Alternatively, you can have a subgroup or the entire team take on a role.

Step #3 Each person takes a turn, in character, generating a list of possible solutions from that perspective. Someone writes these ideas on a flip chart. Encourage group members to become fully involved in their roles. Alternatively, you can have the group, in character, generate ideas at the same time.

You may repeat steps 2-3 for the same challenge question.

Debrief discussion: Did you generate ideas you probably wouldn't have without the role in mind?" This simple question, when answered yes, suggests the value of looking at different roles and stepping into the shoes of different characters.

Creative Collaboration

Story Boarding ....Out of the Box

Purpose: Combine a variety of ideas and possibilities to create a product, story, script, or program design

Time estimate: 30 or more minutes

Supplies needed: A few 5" x 7" cards, about thirty 4" x 6" cards, and about five hundred 3"x5" cards, or different-size Post-it notes, plenty of wall space, markers.

Suggested group size: 3 or more people

Step #1 On each 5" x 7" card or large Post-it note, write a challenge question (for example, "What groups can we target?") and line these up at the top of the wall or board.

Step #2 Have the group non-judgmentally generate a list of headers, general points, categories, or elements of the problem or topic to be considered. Write these on 4" x 6" "header" cards or Post-it notes and place them under the challenge question cards. The team may generate 3-30 headers. Make sure these headers are general and independent categories (for example, age, gender, and income).

Step #3 Have the team non-judgmentally generate ideas for each header and write them on 3" x 5" cards. (For example, age could have subheads of child, teenager, young adult, adult, senior citizen.) Place these "subbers" beneath the appropriate headers (see below for format).

Step #4 Decide as a team which headers to keep.

Step #5 Decide as a team which subbers to keep.

Headers from your board could become problems for the next board, and the subbers could become the new headers, if you were to go further and be more specific.

Example:

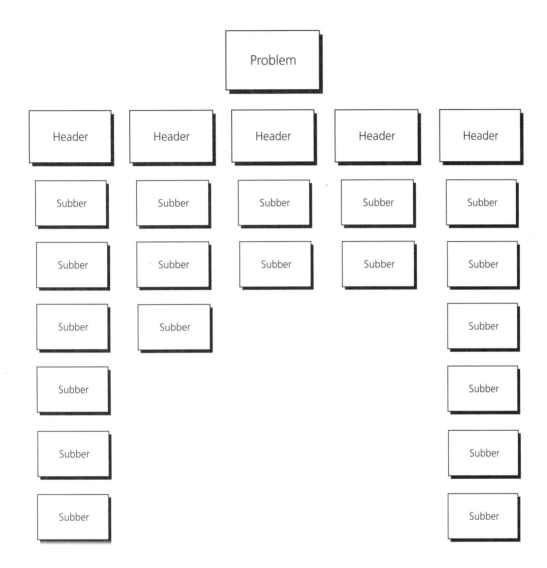

Second Guessing . . . . .Out of the Box

Purpose: Generate lots of ideas by using other ideas as inspiration

Time estimate: 15 or more minutes

Supplies needed: Flip chart and markers, paper, and pen

Suggested group size: 3-15 people

Step #1 Write the challenge question on a flip chart. Answer any clarifying questions about the problem.

Step #2 Group members silently generate solutions on their own and write them down on a piece of paper. Spend only a few minutes on this.

Step #3 Each group member singles out any one of her ideas.

Step #4 One group member comes up with a key word that summarizes her chosen idea and tells the group the key word.

Step #5 The group generates solutions based on the key word in brainstorming fashion (see page 51) for 2-3 minutes only. These second-guessed ideas are written on the flip chart.

Step #6 The person whose word was used to generate the ideas tells the team the original idea on which the key word was based. This idea is also added to the list of second-guessed ideas.

Step #7 The other group members repeat steps 4-6 in turn until everyone has had a chance and you have collected enough ideas.

Hint: You can reduce the amount of time needed in the meeting for this activity by having everyone do steps 1-4 beforehand.

Serial Drawing...................Out of the Box

Purpose: Use visuals to generate ideas

Time estimate: 5-15 minutes

Supplies needed: Flip chart, 8 1/2" x 11" sheet of paper for each person; crayons, markers, or pens for each person

Suggested group size: 3 or more people

Step #1	Everyone takes a sheet of paper and draws a line or a squiggle on it.
Step #2	Everyone passes his marked paper to the next person.
Step #3	That person adds to the mark, starting to create a picture, and then passes again. This goes on for about 3-10 people, creating a drawing on each sheet of paper.
Step#4	State or restate the problem or challenge and ask for any clarifying questions.
Step #5	Ask group members to use the drawing in front of them to inspire and generate new ideas. They can write the ideas on a Post-it note (one idea per note) or call them out in standard brainstorming fashion.

Visual Fit........................Out of the Box

Purpose: Generate breakthrough ideas through pictures

Time estimate: 5 or more minutes

Supplies needed: Flip chart, markers, and pictures (photographs or paintings). You can pick any picture that looks interesting and is clear. The picture should *not* be related to the problem.

Suggested group size: 2 or more people

Step #1 Write the challenge question on the flip chart and answer clarifying questions.

Step #2 Put the challenge question aside. A picture is shown to the group (e.g., a picture of a sailboat).

Step #3 Group members take turns orally describing what they see in the picture. These descriptions are written on the flip chart with no names attached. It is best to write just key words of the description. (For example, for a sailboat picture, key words might include the type of boat, size, color, location, function, etc.)

Step #4 The challenge question is brought back out and the group generates solutions to it using only the descriptions and characteristics of the picture.

Step #5 Repeat steps 2-4, using a new picture, as often as the team desires.

Optional: Try turning the picture upside down or using abstract pictures.

Energizers: Reinvigorate the Group and Increase Focus

90

Attention Quiz........................ **Energizer**

Purpose:

➤ Pay attention to the present

➤ Illustrate how, once you get to know someone, you sometimes stop seeing them

➤ Point out how we do not always see our environment

Time estimate: 5-7 minutes

Supplies needed: None

Suggested group size: 2 or more people

With Partners

Step #1	Team members pair up and sit back-to-back, with eyes closed.
Step #2	The leader asks participants general questions about the physical appearance of their partners, and participants answer these silently to themselves. Then they turn around to see how well they did.

The Room

Step #1	Team members close their eyes.
Step #2	The leader asks them questions about the environment and other members of the group, and participants answer these silently to themselves.
Step #3	Participants open their eyes to see how they did.

Hints: Use about 10 questions. In the pairing version, end by asking the color of their partner's eyes.

Continued...

Examples of questions:
Partners: What color shoes is she wearing? Is he wearing a watch?
Room: What color is the carpeting? How many exits are there? What is Bob wearing around his neck?

Debrief discussion:
What was that like?
How many people got 30%? 50%? 70%? 90%? Anyone get 100%?
Was anyone surprised at how much they remembered?
Was anyone surprised by what they remembered?
When is it important to pay more attention to our environment and each other?

Buffoonery Battle.............. **Energizer**

Purpose:

➤ Let loose and open up the group's creativity

➤ Have fun while increasing the energy in the group

Time estimate: 3-10 minutes

Supplies needed: None

Suggested group size: 4 or more people

Step #1 Divide the group into two teams. (It is okay if the teams are uneven or if there is a team of one.) Decide which team goes first.

Step #2 The first team does everything in its power to make the opposing team laugh. Important rule: Participants cannot touch their opponents (no tickling), so they have to rely on physical and verbal wit. Also ask participants not to use offensive humor.

Step #3 When one person on the receiving team laughs, the teams switch places. Alternatively, when every person on the receiving team laughs, switch places.

Examples of physical and verbal wit:

➤ Make funny faces

➤ Tell a joke

➤ Remind opponents of something they think is funny

➤ Stare into an opponent's face

➤ Walk funny

➤ Talk funny

➤ Say something serious in a nonserious way

➤ Say something nonserious in a serious way

Change..........................

Purpose:

> ➤ Practice observation skills

> ➤ Have fun

Time estimate: 6 minutes

Supplies needed: None

Suggested group size: 2 or more people

Step #1 Team members pair up. One member of the pair is chosen to be "it"; the other becomes the observer.

Step #2 The pairs then turn their backs to each other and the "it" people change *four* things about themselves, such as clothing, hair, jewelry, and other accessories.

Step #3 The pairs turn around to face each other and the observers guess what their partners (the "it" people) have changed about themselves.

Step #4 Alternate roles so the "it" is now the observer and the observer is now the "it."

Examples of changes:

> ➤ Take off a belt

> ➤ Comb your hair differently

> ➤ Put a ring on a different hand

> ➤ Change position of your glasses

> ➤ Put your watch on a different wrist

> ➤ Put a sock on inside out

Hints:

➤ Increase or decrease the number of "changes" to make it more or less difficult. For example, change only two things to make it easier or change six things to make it more difficult.

➤ Give the players ample time to guess the changes.

Debrief discussion: How well did you do? How can being more observant help us in generating ideas?

Company Picnic................ **Energizer**

Purpose:

➤ Illustrate how we all act on perceptions of status within an organization hierarchy

➤ Explore the impact of status on creativity, relationships, sales

➤ Discover when status gets in the way

Time estimate: 15 minutes

Supplies needed: One or more decks of playing cards. Large cards work best.

Suggested group size: 6 or more people

Step #1 Each player is given a card from an ordinary deck of playing cards. Without looking at the card received, each player places his card on his forehead, face out, so that everyone else can see its value.

Step #2 Players mingle for a few minutes, simulating a company picnic. They are to treat one another according to the value of the cards on others' foreheads—an ace represents the highest status person, then king, queen, jack, and so on. The "2" represents the lowest status in the organization. Players are to give each other subtle status clues.

Step #3 At the end of the mingling, players try to line up from lowest to highest card, without looking at their own cards and without helping one another.

Hints:

➤ Notice if there are any mirrors in the room. If so, take steps to help the players avoid looking in the mirrors.

➤ Ask group members not to look at their own cards until after they have lined up. Be subtle! Meet as many people as you can.

Debrief discussion:

What was that like? What did it feel like? How do you feel now?

What clues helped you figure out your card? What clues threw you off?

How did we do? Why were we able to do so well?

What did you learn? How is this like work?

How can status awareness and mastery help?

Where does status get in the way at work?

What can we do to minimize this?

Competitor/Protector............. **Energizer**

Purpose:

➤ Energize the group

➤ Have fun

Time estimate: 3-5 minutes

Supplies needed: None

Suggested group size: 6 or more people

Step #1 Ask the whole group to stand.

Step #2 Ask everyone to randomly and secretly select a person in the room. Then ask participants to silently, in their mind's eye, label their selected person as a "protector."

Step #3 Once again, ask everyone to randomly and secretly select a different person in the room to be labeled "competitor."

Step #4 Tell group members that when you say "Go," they are to move around the room, trying to keep their "protector" on a straight line between their "competitor" and themselves. Instruct players not to move or grab their fellow players and that running is not allowed.

Step #5 To end each round, yell "Freeze!" and ask the players: "Who's properly protected right now?"

Variations: Competitor/Competitor: Group members label themselves "protectors," and place themselves between two individuals they have labeled as "competitors."

Hint: Play several times so different patterns emerge.

Debrief discussion: What was that like for you?

Count To... •••••••••••••••••••••••••••••••••••••

Energizer

Purpose:

➤ Engage people

➤ Refocus team members away from arguing

➤ Make a point about not talking over one another

➤ Create synergy and share control

➤ Focus the group before visioning

Time estimate: 5-15 minutes

Supplies needed: None

Suggested group size: 5 or more people

Step #1	Ask group members to form a circle.
Step #2	Count aloud one at a time from 1 to 10; anyone can say "1," anyone else can say "2," and so on. The only rules are:

    1) No one person can say two consecutive numbers.

    2) The group cannot use any kind of system.

    3) When two or more people speak at once, the count goes back to 1.

Variations:

➤ Count to 20   ➤ Count with eyes closed

➤ Count from A to Z

Hint: If you hear two or more people start to say a number just say "1" and we'll start over again. We won't argue about whether or not it happened.

Debrief discussion: How were we able to make it? Did anyone not say a number? (If this exercise is at the end of a section or workshop, skip the processing so the group can end on a big cheer.)

Name Go.............................. **Energizer**

Purpose: Learn one another's names

Time estimate: 7-10 minutes

Supplies needed: None

Suggested group size: 5 or more people

Step #1 Ask group members to form a circle.

Step #2 Pick someone (A) to go first.

Step #3 Person A starts by making eye contact with another person and calling out that person's first name. That person (B) replies "Go!" giving person A the green light to move across the circle to take B's position. Before A has reached her, B vacates her position by repeating the pattern: selecting another person (C), calling his name, and getting the "Go!" to move to take over C's position. This pattern continues so that all group members move positions several times. Instruct players to walk; don't run.

Hints: This game is difficult! Players will instinctively start moving to their new positions before getting the "Go," but they must wait until they hear "Go" before moving. This is harder than it seems. Gently correct and re-explain as necessary.

Variations: Name Game: Instead of shouting "Go," players say their own name before selecting someone else's name.

Debrief discussion: What was that like?
What problems came up?
How did you feel?

Clapping............................. **Energizer**

Purpose: Have fun and create synergy and energy

Time estimate: 5-8 minutes

Supplies: none

Suggested group size: 5 or more people

Step #1	Ask group members to form a circle.
Step #2	Ask for a person to go first.
Step #3	The first person turns to the person on her right and claps her hands (a single clap or a series in any rhythm), making eye contact while doing so.
Step #4	The receiver then turns to the person on his right, makes eye contact, and passes the same clap to that person. If a series of claps is being passed, the player must try to match the rhythm or tempo he was just given. The passing continues from person to person around the circle. The clapping could reach lightning speed where all players are clapping almost simultaneously. This would be a good time to stop.

Variations:

➤ Tell group members that they may decide to clap back to the neighbor who just passed to them. Try it and notice how disruptive this can be.

➤ When receiving a clap, first clap back to the sender, then turn to your neighbor to pass it on.

➤ Pass claps either low (bending down) or high (above your head), or combine the two variations.

➤ Try clapping twice, three times, or four times when you pass to the next person.

Hint: Start the group slowly and have them pick up speed.

Simon Does Not Say............... **Energizer**

Purpose: Encourage nonconformist thinking

Time estimate: 5 or more minutes

Supplies needed: None

Suggested group size: 5 or more people

> This game is just like Simon Says, only you do not do the action when Simon says.
>
> **Step #1** Pick someone to be "Simon," the leader.
>
> **Step #2** Simon directs the others to do something by stating a command. When Simon prefaces his statement with "Simon Says" and a group member obeys the command, that person is out of the game. If, however, the leader omits the preface "Simon Says" and just makes the command and players follow the command, they stay in the game.

Examples of activities:

➤ Jump up and down

➤ Say a specific word

➤ Walk a certain way

Hints: The faster you do this game, the harder it is. Allow others to have the chance to play "Simon."

Story Name Game................. **Energizer**

Purpose:

➤ Get players to learn something new about one another and their names

➤ Break the mind-set of thinking we know everything about our co-workers and thus taking each other for granted

Time estimate: 4-10 minutes

Supplies needed: None

Suggested group size: 4 or more people

Step #1 Ask group members to form a circle.

Step #2 Starting with the coach, each player says his full name and briefly tells the story behind his name, such as how he got the name, the meaning of the name, nicknames, and so on. Take about 30 seconds per player.

Hints:

➤ Use with groups in which most players already know each other

➤ Tell players that the stories do not have to be funny or clever

Debrief discussion: Ask for players' observations. Ask if players learned something new about one another. Ask if any players were rehearsing what they were going to say, and mention that this is natural to do. Point out, however, that they are the experts in their own name so they do not need to preplan their story. We get in the habit of thinking ahead.

You .... Energizer

Purpose:

➤ Enliven members of the group

➤ Get people focused, present, and tuned in to the group

➤ Have fun

Time estimate: 15 minutes

Supplies needed: None

Suggested group size: 5 or more people

Step #1 Ask group members to form a circle and raise their right hands.

Step #2 Have the group establish a pattern by asking someone to point to another person with their right hand and say "you." That person then points to another person and says "you" and so on until everyone is pointing at someone. Players should pay attention to and memorize who is pointing at them (the person from whom they'll be receiving the "you") and at whom they are pointing (the person to whom they'll be passing the "you"). When players are familiar with the pattern, ask them to repeat the exercise without pointing.

Step #3 Create a new pattern using words or concepts (each participant selects a unique word) from a category, such as vegetables, cars, or colors, rather than the word "you." Again, players should pay attention to who is giving them a word and to whom they are passing their own word. This pattern also is memorized and repeated.

Step #4 The two patterns are then executed at the same time simply by having players look at each other and say the word (players should not point). If the person to whom a player is passing a word is not paying attention, the passer must keep looking at him and saying the word until the person receives it and passes to the next person. The group continues to create and add patterns on top of each other.

Variations:

➤ Pass participants' names around the circle, either clockwise or counterclockwise, as one of the patterns.

➤ On the last go-round, have participants move on the "you," taking the place of the person they point to.

Hints: Watch for the "you." Listen for the category. Remember to whom you pointed. Remember who pointed at you. This is hard. Keep sending your word until it has been passed along.

Debrief discussion:

What was that like? What did it feel like? How do you feel now?

What worked? What made it hard? What could help?

What did you learn?

How is this like work?

Resources

Books

De Bono, Edward. *Six Thinking Hats*. NY: Little, Brown and Company, 1999.

Goman, Carol Kinsey. *Creativity in Business, Revised Edition*. Menlo Park, CA: Crisp Publications, 2000.

Hackett, Donald and Charles L. Martin. *Facilitation Skills for Team Leaders*. Menlo Park, CA: Crisp Publications, 1993.

Haynes, Marion E. *Effective Meeting Skills, Revised Edition*. Menlo Park, CA: Crisp Publications, 1997.

Johnstone, Keith. Impro: *Improvisation and the Theatre*. NY: Theatre Arts Books, 1989.

Kaner, Sam, Lenny Lind, Catherine Toldi, Sarah Fisk, and Duane Berger. *Facilitator's Guide to Participatory Decision-Making*. British Columbia, Canada: New Society Publishers, 1996.

Kearny, Lynn. *Graphics for Presenters*. Menlo Park, CA: Crisp Publications, 1996.

Koberg, Dan and Jim Bagnall. *Universal Traveler*. Menlo Park, CA: Crisp Publications, 1991.

Michalko, Michael. *Thinkertoys: A Handbook of Business Creativity*. Berkeley, CA: Ten Speed Press, 1991.

Michalko, Michael. *Thinkpak: A Brainstorming Card Deck*. Berkeley, CA: Ten Speed Press, 1994.

Miller, William C. *The Creative Edge: Fostering Innovation Where You Work*. Cambridge, MA: Perseus Publishing, 1990.

Miller, William C. and Robert B. Shapiro. *Flash of Brilliance: Inspiring Creativity Where You Work*. Cambridge, MA: Perseus Publishing, 1998.

Pokras, Sandy. *Rapid Team Deployment*. Menlo Park, CA: Crisp Publications, 1995.

Thiagarajan, Sivasailam and Glenn M. Parker. *Teamwork and Teamplay: Games and Activities for Building and Training Teams*. San Francisco, CA: Jossey-Bass, 1999.

Wujec, Tom. *Five Star Mind: Games and Exercises to Stimulate Your Creativity and Imagination*. NY: Main Street Books, August 1995.

Other

Aha! & Ha ha ha Cards: Creative Activities to Play with your Children, Bruce Honig, Honig IdeaGuides, 2002. Write to products@honigideaguides.com.

Aha! Cards: Inspiring Your Team to Creative Action, Bruce Honig, IdeaGuides, 2002, www.ideaguides.com/aha.html

CREATE: The Game that Challenges and Expands Your Creativity, Bruce Honig, Honig IdeaGuides, 1985, www. ideashoppe.net

Innovation Styles Assessment, William C. Miller. www.creativeadvantage.com/ what_are_innovation_styles.htm

Juicers Flip-Cards, Alain Rostain, Creative Advantage, www.creativeadvantage.com, 2001, www.creativeadvantage.com/fc-juicers.htm

Meeting Effectiveness Flip Cards, Bruce Honig, Honig IdeaGuides, 2002, www.creativeadvantage.com/fc-meeting_effectiveness.htm

Web sites

International Association of Facilitators: www.iaf-world.org

InnovationNetwork: www.thinksmart.com

Improv Encyclopedia Homepage at www.humanpingpongball.com

108

NOTES

Now Available From

Books•Videos•CD-ROMs•Computer-Based Training Products

If you enjoyed this book, we have great news for you.
There are over 200 books available in the *Fifty-Minute*™ *Series*.
To request a free full-line catalog, contact your local distributor or
Crisp Learning
1200 Hamilton Court
Menlo Park, CA 94025
1-800-442-7477
www.crisplearning.com

Subject Areas Include:

Management
Human Resources
Communication Skills
Personal Development
Marketing/Sales
Organizational Development
Customer Service/Quality
Computer Skills
Small Business and Entrepreneurship
Adult Literacy and Learning
Life Planning and Retirement

Creative Collaboration

CRISP WORLDWIDE DISTRIBUTION

English language books are distributed worldwide. Major international distributors include:

ASIA/PACIFIC

Australia/New Zealand: In Learning, PO Box 1051, Springwood QLD, Brisbane, Australia 4127   Tel: 61-7-3-841-2286, Facsimile: 61-7-3-841-1580
ATTN: Messrs. Richard/Robert Gordon

Hong Kong/Mainland China: Crisp Learning Solutions, 18/F Honest Motors Building 9-11 Leighton Road, Causeway Bay, Hong Kong   Tel: 852-2915-7119,
Facsimile: 852-2865-2815 ATTN: Ms. Grace Lee

Indonesia: Pt Lutan Edukasi, Citra Graha, 7th Floor, Suite 701A, Jl. Jend.
Gato Subroto Kav. 35-36, Jakarta 12950 Indonesia Tel: 62-21-527-9060/527-9061 Facsimile: 62-21-527-9062 ATTN: Mr. Suwardi Luis

Japan: Phoenix Associates, Believe Mita Bldg., 8th Floor 3-43-16 Shiba, Minato-ku, Tokyo 105-0014, Japan   Tel: 81-3-5427-6231, Facsimile: 81-3-5427-6232
ATTN: Mr. Peter Owans

Malaysia, Philippines, Singapore: Epsys Pte Ltd., 540 Sims Avenue #04-01, Sims Avenue Centre, 387603, Singapore   Tel: 65-747-1964, Facsimile: 65-747-0162 ATTN: Mr. Jack Chin

CANADA

Crisp Learning Canada, 60 Briarwood Avenue, Mississauga, ON L5G 3N6 Canada
Tel: 905-274-5678, Facsimile: 905-278-2801 ATTN: Mr. Steve Connolly

EUROPEAN UNION

England: Flex Learning Media, Ltd., 9-15 Hitchin Street,
Baldock, Hertfordshire, SG7 6AL, England
Tel: 44-1-46-289-6000, Facsimile: 44-1-46-289-2417   ATTN: Mr. David Willetts

INDIA

Multi-Media HRD, Pvt. Ltd., National House, Floor 1, 6 Tulloch Road,
Appolo Bunder, Bombay, India 400-039 Tel: 91-22-204-2281,
Facsimile: 91-22-283-6478 ATTN: Messrs. Ajay Aggarwal/ C.L. Aggarwal

SOUTH AMERICA

Mexico: Grupo Editorial Iberoamerica, Nebraska 199, Col. Napoles, 03810 Mexico, D.F.
Tel: 525-523-0994, Facsimile: 525-543-1173   ATTN: Señor Nicholas Grepe

SOUTH AFRICA

Corporate: Learning Resources, PO Box 2806, Parklands, Johannesburg 2121, South Africa, Tel: 27-21-531-2923, Facsimile: 27-21-531-2944 ATTN: Mr. Ricky Robinson

MIDDLE EAST

Edutech Middle East, L.L.C., PO Box 52334, Dubai U.A.E.
Tel: 971-4-359-1222, Facsimile: 971-4-359-6500   ATTN: Mr. A.S.F. Karim